$\sqrt{\dfrac{\text{The}\,(\text{Theory})\,\text{of}}{\text{Accountability}^2}}$

Easy vs Hard
Simple vs Complex

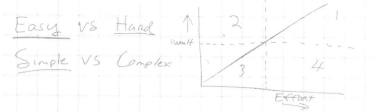

$E = mc^2$
E = Experience
M = Mindset
C = Commitment

$\sqrt{\text{The (Theory) of}}$
Accountability^2

Building a **Truly Accountable, High-Performance, High-Growth Life** for Yourself and Your Organization

Commitment & Consistency

As a Leader, what "E" are you trying to maximize?

This is simple
It takes hard work
Commitment

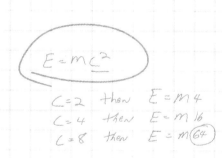

$E = mc^2$

C = 2   then   E = m 4
C = 4   then   E = m 16
C = 8   then   E = m (64)

BY SAM SILVERSTEIN

AUTHOR OF **NO MORE EXCUSES, NO MATTER WHAT, & I AM ACCOUNTABLE**

Productivity ≠ Accountability

Accountability ⟹ Productivity

*To that small still voice that comes to everyone
and those people who listen and take action on what they hear.*

Acknowledgments

MY BOOKS ARE A TEAM EFFORT. Without everyone's hard work and commitment, *The Theory of Accountability* would not have been possible.

I would like to thank:

David Wildasin and the entire team at Sound Wisdom for their tireless efforts. You get behind my projects, make them look great, and make it possible to deliver important messages to the world. Thank you for your commitment to my writing.

My personal editor Cara Wordsmith, Ltd. works enthusiastically to help make my books the very best they can be. It is a joy to work closely on projects like this.

And to you the reader – thank you for not only reading my books but also your emails and communication on social media about how you have been impacted by what I write. I love hearing from you about the difference you make with these ideas.

Thank you.

Published and distributed by:
SOUND WISDOM
P.O. Box 310
Shippensburg, PA 17257-0310
717-530-2122

info@soundwisdom.com

www.soundwisdom.com

Cover/jacket design by Geoff Silverstein

ISBN 13 TP: 978-1-64095-275-1

ISBN 13 eBook: 978-1-64095-276-8

For Worldwide Distribution, Printed in the U.S.A.

1 2 3 4 5 6 7 8 / 25 24 23 22 21

Contents

Read This First 13

Part One: What Is Accountability? **15**

1.   The Way We Think 17

2.   The Theory of Accountability .27

Part Two: Creating the Experience. **31**

3.   The Three Mentors 33

4.   The Future Begins Right Now 45

5.   The Moment of Truth Is the Moment
You Move Beyond What Is Comfortable 53

6.   Excuse or Possibility? 61

7.   Purpose and Experience 69

8.   Take the Time 77

9.   Living Your Purpose Means
Pursuing Fulfillment, Not Happiness 83

10.   Living Your Purpose Means Creating the Future 87

11.   Living Your Purpose Means
       Recognizing Excuses...and Moving Beyond Them 91

12.   Put What You Have Learned
       about the "E" in $E=mc^2$ into Practice! 95

Part Three: Stepping into the Mindset. 99

13.   The "m" in $E=mc^2$. 101

14.   Three Accountable Mindsets, Three Toxic Mindsets . . 105

15.   Accountable Mindsets Take Practice;
       Toxic Mindsets Are Easy. 119

16.   What We Need to Notice about Mindset 123

17.   Four Simple Things You Can Do
       to Ensure Your Mindset Is Accountable 131

18.   What Do You Really Believe? 135

19.   Put What You Have Learned
       about the "m" in $E=mc^2$ into Practice!. 141

Part Four: Commitment—Swinging the Hammer. 147

20.   The "c" in $E=mc^2$: Commitment. 149

21. Exponential Commitment 159

22. Put Your Commitment Where Your Mouth Is! 163

23. How Big a Life Do You Want to Lead? 167

24. Who Are You, Really? 175

25. Put What You Have Learned
     about the "c" in E=mc^2 into Practice! 179

26. The Values Factor 183

Appendix

     Summary of Accountability Points from This Book . . .187

     About the Author 201

Read This First

IT WAS 5:00 ON A SATURDAY MORNING, and all I could do was toss and turn in bed. I had been awake, restless for half an hour. I just could not fall back asleep. I kept thinking about the strange, impossible sound that had awoken me. An unseen voice had stirred me.

It was as if someone had walked to the side of my bed, leaned down, and whispered right in my ear: "$E=mc^2$."

I had scanned the room. There was no one there. Now the problem was that I could not get that formula out of my head and I could not fall back asleep. Although I am no expert in physics, I knew well enough what that famous formula developed by Albert Einstein stood for. What I could not figure out was why it was being given to me at this point in time—and what, exactly, I was supposed to do with it. At 5:15 I gave up, slipped out of bed without waking my wife Renee, and went downstairs to my office.

Once in my office, I did not go to my computer as I usually would, but rather I stood in front of my whiteboard and wrote down the formula I couldn't seem to get out of my head:

$$E=mc^2$$

For the next ten minutes I just stared at it. Then, seized by sudden inspiration, I began to write. Once I started, I continued to write and draw on that whiteboard for the next 45 minutes. When I was done, I had produced the outline of what felt like an entire PhD dissertation on the formula that had been whispered to me by that unseen speaker. But this dissertation was not about physics. It was about accountability.

I stepped back from the board and looked at what I had put there. I saw a maze of words, numbers, and drawings that looked as though they had been created by someone else. Yet I knew that it had been my black marker that had drawn the ideas I was now looking at. I took it all in. It was at that moment that I realized the importance of what had been given to me. What I had written down was the key to designing the future you want for yourself and/or your organization…and achieving that future.

It was all crystal clear in my mind now. What I had put on that white board was not the Theory of Relativity that Albert Einstein had first discovered a century ago, but rather something that I, in that moment, dubbed the Theory of Accountability. The ideas I was supposed to put on that whiteboard in the hour before dawn would not let me sleep, and I have never been so grateful for a case of insomnia in my life. This book is based on those ideas.

If you want a copy of
the original whiteboard drawing, go to

www.samsilverstein.com/emc2.

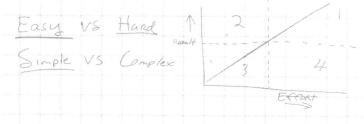

Easy vs Hard

Simple vs Complex

Result ↑ | Effort →
(graph with 2, 1, 3, 4 regions)

$$E = mc^2$$

E = Experience

M = Mindset

C = Commitment

Part One

(What Is Accountability?)

Commitment & Consistency

As a Leader, what "E" are you trying to maximize?

This is simple
It takes hard work
Commitment

Productivity ≠ Accountability

Accountability ⇒ Productivity

Chapter One

The Way We Think

"Life is like a camera. Just focus on what's important." —Dorothy Smith

MY JOB FOR THE PAST THREE DECADES has been to help people have powerful, transformative conversations about accountability—conversations that create sustainable, measurable improvements in both personal and organizational performance. These conversations usually begin with a question that is, in my experience, too often overlooked: *What is accountability...and how does it work?*

Initially, the goal of these conversations is for us to become more accountable individually, but ultimately they allow us to build a more accountable organization. Then, through the organization we build and support together, we can contribute to building greater accountability in our community. During these conversations about accountability, I ask people to think differently. I want to ask you to think differently, too, as you read this book, because I believe that many of us have been trained to think of accountability in one direction, when in reality, it is pointing us in a very different direction.

> **If we want to make accountability a daily reality in our life, in our team, and in our organization, we must change the way we think.**

By the way, the text in the box you just read is what I call an Accountability Point, a particularly important insight or action item for people whose aim is to become a Master of Accountability. These Accountability Points also appear in a special Appendix at the end of the book, so you can consult them easily when you want to revisit or reinforce the concepts I am sharing with you in these pages.

ASK DIFFERENT QUESTIONS

A big part of the conversation I have with leaders who are seeking to improve accountability in their organizations is challenging them to ask different questions than the ones they are used to asking. One of those new questions is: *How can accountability produce better results for me and my organization?*

Let's face it. At many organizations, the way leaders and others approach accountability *is not* producing better results. Using the idea of accountability to manipulate people only produces fear, resentment, dysfunction, and disengagement.

So here are some questions for leaders:

- What do you think happens to a member of the team when they hear the words "I am going to hold you accountable"?

- Does saying, "I am going to hold you accountable" make team members more resourceful—or does it make them more likely to shut down?

- Could saying, "I am going to hold you accountable" be interpreted as a threat?

- What happens when you start a relationship off with a threat?

- How do you think starting the relationship off with a threat makes people feel? Does it make them feel valued...or manipulated?

- Does being threatened make people more creative—or less creative?

- Does being threatened make people more transparent with you—or less likely to speak up when they see a problem on the horizon?

- Is the experience of "being held accountable" something *you* would volunteer for?

When I ask leaders to think differently about accountability, what I am asking them to consider is this:

> All my research, over a period of more than three decades now, has shown me that everything we have been told about accountability is wrong.

If we are leaders, the odds are high that we have been looking at this from the wrong angle for a long time. Yes, we all want our people to do their jobs. We want them to keep their commitments. We want them to get their work done. We want them to work more efficiently. But you know what? In our organizations today, the real problem is not the people.

The real problem is how leaders *see* their people. That is the key. We need to change how we look at our people and how we think about accountability. This brings to mind an important observation from the great theoretical physicist Albert Einstein, who observed:

> "We cannot solve our problems with the same thinking we used when we created them."
> —Albert Einstein

This is *not* simply good advice for theoretical physicists. It is good advice for human beings—and particularly for those who are leaders or aspiring leaders. If we see accountability simply as a means of manipulating our people into doing more, we will reinforce a destructive cultural cycle. And that is what I see out there. I see leaders trying to "hold their people accountable," trying to use the words "accountable" and "accountability" as weapons to change the behavior of the members of their team. That does not work. It does not make people want to show up early, stay late, or come up with breakthroughs in production, design, or execution. All it does is make them wary of the leaders who are trying to manipulate them.

More to the point, manipulation is not what accountability is really about.

> It is the responsibility of the leader to create an environment that inspires and prioritizes accountability.

If we have a leadership role, it is our responsibility to create an environment that inspires and prioritizes accountability so that people *want* to be their best and *want* to contribute at the highest possible levels, without anyone ever threatening them, cajoling them, or manipulating them. By the way, this same dynamic holds true in a family setting, just as it does in a business setting.

Very often, this kind of change means leaders must modify the very foundations of the working relationships they have created. They must change from "I am going to hold you accountable" to "How can I help you be successful?" This opens the relationship instead of closing it. As Einstein might put it, this new approach changes the thinking we used when we created the problems in the first place.

When we start to see people differently, we start to treat them differently and we commit to them differently. When that happens, we get a different result. This principle applies not just to people with formal leadership positions within organizations; it applies to everyone who aims to establish leadership in their own life.

THE CULTURAL CHALLENGE: WHAT IS ACCOUNTABILITY?

At the organizational level, which is the level I am usually asked to help with, the kind of change I am talking about presents itself, first and foremost, as a cultural change. What I end up proposing to teams and those who lead them is a radical transition in how leaders see their people, a transition that creates an organizational culture that actually *inspires* accountability in team members.

> Here is the thing we often overlook about accountability: It can never be mandated. It can only be inspired.

So let's go back to our initial question. What *is* accountability, really? Only by addressing this question can we make accountability a reality in our culture.

I have asked this question of tens of thousands of people at organizations all around the world. I have heard thousands of answers in response. And I have consulted more dictionaries, white papers, and business articles than I care to calculate in search of the best, most practical definition. I have never found an answer to this essential question better than this one:

> Accountability is keeping your commitments to people.

That is it. That is what accountability means. If we can just keep our eye on that definition, we will be in the position to transform our relationships, our teams, our organization, and, eventually, the community in which we live. We really can use accountability to create massive, measurable improvements in all of those realms of life.

But we need to understand that those improvements do not happen automatically. Before we can hope to contribute at the highest level, we must accept that for years, we have confused things. We have done a masterful job of connecting two words that really should not be connected: responsibility and accountability.

> **We are responsible for things,**
> **but we are accountable to people.**

When we make the mistake of confusing accountability and responsibility, we lose sight of the human relationship and we focus instead on the transaction. We begin to see and treat people as a means to an end. We make the relationship all about getting things done. That is a cultural disaster and a major failure of leadership.

No matter how much leaders and others may talk about *valuing people* or *putting people first*, people can always tell when they are being used as a means to an end. People know when someone values the outcome more than the relationship. People realize when leadership has failed to honor the most important commitments. In short, they can tell when someone is not accountable.

The conversation about accountable leadership, whether it is to be expressed in the context of a work team or any other aspect of the human experience, can be boiled down to four words: *accountability starts with us.*

Do we want people to tell us the truth? Then we must first make a commitment to the truth.

Do we want people to act with integrity? Then we must first make a commitment to identify what we value and then live what we value.

Do we want people to think and act like a team? Then we must first make a commitment to "It's all of us."

Do we want people to respond loyally, effectively, and resourcefully when times are tough? Then we must first make a commitment to stand with people when all hell breaks loose in their lives.

Do we want people to use resources responsibly? Then we must first make a commitment to sound financial principles.

Do we want our family, our team, or our organization to achieve great things? Then we must make a commitment to helping others to achieve their potential and be their best.

Do we want people to make powerful contributions that grow in both value and impact over time? Then we must first make a commitment to the faults and failures, as well as the opportunities and successes.

Do we want people to move heaven and earth to keep their commitments to us and tell us well in advance when they face an unexpected obstacle that keeps them from doing what they said they would do? Then we must make a commitment to make our word our bond.

Do we want people to innovate? Then we must treat employees well, ensure they are valued, and ensure they feel safe speaking up with new ideas—and that means making a commitment to a physically and emotionally safe workplace.

Do we want our people to show up inspired and proud to be part of our family, our organization, our community? Then we must make a commitment to a good reputation.

Do we want our customers to be treated so well that they feel great about doing business with us? Then we need to treat our employees so well that they feel great about working for us—so great that they brag about the organization to friends and family.

We have to stop thinking about holding someone else accountable. That is the big shift. As leaders, we want to move this discussion to the next level, the level of helping our people to be accountable because we are modeling that accountability first and inspiring accountability in others.

> When it comes to accountability, we get only what we give. In organizational terms, accountability always starts with accountable leadership. And accountability is the ultimate competitive advantage.

Chapter Two

The Theory
of Accountability

"Blame is the water in which many dreams and relationships drown." —Steve Maraboli

"HOW ACCOUNTABLE AM I?" This is a question we should never stop asking ourselves.

Accountability, as we have seen, is keeping your commitments to people. Accountability never stops. Accountability is proactive. Accountability requires both conscious effort and continuous action over time. The minute you stop asking yourself how well you are keeping your commitments, the minute you stop taking action to strengthen relationships, accountability fades.

Often, I will hear leaders say something like this: "Sure, I'm accountable. I make sure the paycheck shows up every two weeks for every person in this organization. That's my responsibility. And I make sure it happens like clockwork. If that's not accountability, what is?" And for them, that really is where the discussion about accountability stops.

Can you see the problem with that kind of thinking?

Remember: We are *responsible* for things. We are *accountable* to people. And while ensuring the payroll runs smoothly and reliably certainly *affects* the quality of the relationship, it is not actually accountability, because on its own, it does not support any truly personal commitment *within* the relationship.

Accountability is *personal*. It is all about *relational* commitments—things people follow through on to ensure the relationship with another person strengthens over time. Responsibility, on the other hand, is *tactical*. Is making sure people get paid a commitment? Sure. So is making sure your electric bill gets paid. That is a tactical commitment. It does not imply any meaningful connection between human beings.

> Tactical commitments are not enough. If there is no relational commitment anywhere, then there is no accountability.

Tactical commitments are spoken, for the most part. Relational commitments do not need to be spoken and are more powerful when they are not spoken, as long as the actions prove them. Actions carry far more value than words. If you are a leader, the most important commitment you fulfill is *not* the commitment to check tactical responsibilities off the to-do list (although that definitely matters). Your most important commitments are the ones that directly affect the quality of your *personal* relationship with the individual employee! For instance:

- Your commitment to live the values. (At the individual level, this means your personal values. At the organizational level, this means the company's values.)

- Your commitment to "my word is my bond." (If for some reason there is a problem with the paycheck and you tell

THE THEORY OF ACCOUNTABILITY

the employee that you are going to take care of it, don't you want the employee to be able to trust that you're going to be as good as your word?)

- Your commitment to stand by the employee. (Not just when there is a problem, not just when all hell breaks loose in the employee's life, but at all times.)

Accountability really is all about keeping *relational* commitments: the commitment to the truth, the commitment to "It's all of us," the commitment to live what we value, and so on. And the most inspiring people, in my experience, are the ones who never stop asking themselves how they can strengthen those relational commitments.

Again: If the only evidence for accountability you can point to is transactional, *that is not accountability.* It is responsibility. Those are two entirely different things. And by the way, if you are a leader and you are *not* fulfilling your tactical commitments to your people, that means you are not fulfilling the core requirements of the job... and you should find something else to do! (This principle applies to everyone, by the way, not just to people who have formal leadership positions.)

THE ACCOUNTABILITY EQUATION

I believe there are three critical factors that determine the level of accountability in our life, our organization, and our community—three areas where we are constantly challenged to follow Einstein's advice and change our thinking so that we can produce a different and better outcome for ourselves, the people we work with, and the entire human family. When we ask ourselves *How accountable am I?*, these three areas are where we need to look first to find the answers:

- The **Experience** we create for ourselves and others, meaning the future we make a conscious choice to step into.

- The **Mindset** we adopt in support of that experience, meaning the beliefs we have about the people around us, the world, and ourselves.

- The **Commitment** we take on. This means the persistent, relentless action we undertake in support of the experience we are creating, our beliefs, and our relationships.

Each of these must be aligned with our larger purpose as individuals or as organizations.

This can be expressed in a simple formula to describe the steps required to make accountability a daily reality in our life:

> The *Experience* we create is the result of the *Mindset* we embrace and the exponential impact of our Commitment.
> Or: $E = mc^2$

Accountability is not a way of doing. Accountability is a way of thinking about people through the lens of *Experience, Mindset, and Commitment.*

This formula I have just shared with you is true for everyone, and understanding it is the key to establishing leadership in your own life and contributing powerfully to the lives of others.

If that possibility intrigues you, read on.

Easy vs Hard
Simple vs Complex

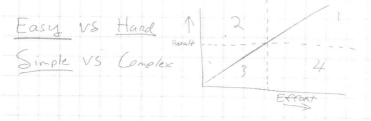

$E = mc^2$
E = Experience
M = Mindset
C = Commitment

Part Two

(Creating the Experience)

Commitment ? Consistency

As a Leader, what "E"
are you trying to maximize?

This is simple
It takes hard work
Commitment

Productivity ≠ Accountability

Accountability ⇒ Productivity

Chapter Three

The Three Mentors

"The mediocre mentor tells. The good mentor explains. The greatest mentors inspire." —Lucia Ballas-Traynor

CREATING THE EXPERIENCE means creating a clear mental picture of the compelling future that you want to step into—a picture that engages, excites, and motivates you. This step is essential. It is the foundation of accountability, and it takes practice.

> Creating the Experience is the foundation of accountability, and it takes practice. For most of us, it also takes outside help.

What I have noticed over the years, in working as an accountability advisor and consultant for both teams and individuals, is that most people—not all, but most—need a little help with this critical initial step. For the vast majority of us, learning to create the Experience does not come naturally, and mastering this step means enlisting the help and guidance of a mentor.

Not only that—once we have set the Experience once or twice, we may still need a little help from a mentor. This is true for people with deep experience in accountability, and it is certainly true for those just learning the process. Why is this so? Because we do not know what we are truly capable of. We are deeply limited by our own sense of what is possible in our lives. So we create, and step into, an Experience that limits us, rather than one that expands our horizons and our capacity to contribute.

Here is one of my favorite examples of how people create a limited Experience, one that does not reflect what they are truly capable of.

In the years immediately following World War II, a young Navy lieutenant, who had been badly injured in the war and who had a deep aversion to public speaking, was persuaded by his family to run for Congress. He was, however, deeply skeptical about his own campaign. The Navy man insisted that he was not cut out for politics, because he considered himself a terrible public speaker. He told people repeatedly that this was the case. That was him creating a limited Experience for himself and everyone in his circle.

> All too often, we create a limited experience for ourselves and those in our circle.

With the help of a mentor who insisted that he had the potential to become not just a good, but a great public speaker, the young Navy veteran began to practice and improve. His early speeches were awkward.

But as he received coaching from his mentor, he learned to draw his audience in, modulate his voice, pose questions and leave them unanswered for a while, and tell true stories about his own experiences in the war in a way that touched people's hearts.

His mentor helped him every step of the way. As a result, the young man's confidence grew, and he began to envision himself as a great public speaker—which, it turned out, he was!

That was the future his mentor helped him to envision and step into. That was the Experience the young man ultimately chose to set for himself. He would not have chosen it for himself, or even believed it to be possible, without the prompting of his mentor.

The young Congressional candidate's name was John F. Kennedy. His mentor was his father, Joe. John F. Kennedy won, not only that race for Congress, but every election in which he competed. Along the way, he earned a well-deserved reputation as one of the truly great orators of the twentieth century. And he did it with the help of a mentor.

Here is how Kennedy's sister, Eunice, recalls the working relationship between the two men: "Many a night when [Kennedy] would come over to see Daddy after a speech, he'd be feeling rather down, admitting that the speech hadn't really gone very well or believing that his delivery had put the people in the front row fast asleep. 'What do you mean?' Father would immediately ask. 'Why I talked to Mr. X and Mrs. Y on the phone right after they got home and they told me they were sitting right in the front row and that it was a fine speech.' ...Father would go on to elicit from Jack what he thought he could change to make it better next time. I can still see the two of them sitting together, analyzing the entire speech and talking about the pace of delivery."[1]

---

1. Doris Kearns Goodwin, *The Fitzgeralds and the Kennedys: An American Saga* (New York: St. Martin's Press, 1987), 707.

What were they focused on? A new future; a new, improved experience: *how to make it better next time.* This is what creating the Experience looks like in action. We break through preconceptions and self-imposed barriers. Creating the Experience is transformative because we learn from setbacks and recalibrate based on what we have learned from them.

Choosing the Experience we want sets us on the path to the future we want to live. And learning to make that choice is essential if we aim to make a lasting positive impact on our own life and the lives of others.

ANOTHER EXAMPLE OF CHOOSING AND CREATING A POWERFUL EXPERIENCE

Coincidentally, in the very same year, 1946, a fateful conversation took place between another young man and his mentor. This conversation led to another, even more powerful instance of two people creating a new future and a new, improved Experience. It took place in Brooklyn, New York, between Brooklyn Dodgers president Branch Rickey and Negro leagues star Jackie Robinson.

Now, I realize that you may already be familiar with the broad outlines of the story of Jackie Robinson, the brave and brilliant athlete who in 1947, a year after this discussion, became the first African American to play in Major League Baseball since the 1880s. Most people know who Robinson was and how huge a story his rise to the big leagues was. I have a question for you, though: What Experience do you think Robinson chose, and began to step into, on that day in 1946 when he first met with Rickey in Rickey's Brooklyn office? What future were they creating together?

You might be tempted to say, "Getting into the major leagues, and thereby breaking the color barrier." That would be an *incomplete* answer. It would not be technically wrong. But it would not match up with the reality of either man's life and choices and sacrifices. And it would not accurately describe the future they envisioned.

Both Robinson and Rickey were aiming much, much higher than simply getting a Black man on a big-league roster. Each man knew that integrating baseball was a crucial psychological milestone for the United States as a whole. Each man knew just how daunting the job would be. Each man knew the devastating impact on the country as a whole, and on African Americans specifically, if Rickey's gambit failed. Each man also knew that that was exactly what the vast majority of big-league owners, players, and power brokers wanted when it came to integrating baseball, and integrating America as a whole: failure.

A very brief overview of the personal history of each man is in order here. Rickey had been quietly laying the groundwork for the desegregation of Brooklyn's rosters for at least four years, because he had been sickened for decades by his own first-hand observations of racism, both on the field and off. While managing the Ohio Wesleyan University team in 1904, Rickey watched in disgust as a Black player, Charles Thomas, was reduced to tears at being refused a room in the hotel where the rest of the team was staying. Although Rickey managed to circumvent the rules to get Thomas into the hotel that night, the incident stayed with Rickey. He was later quoted as saying, "I may not be able to do something about racism in every field, but I can sure do something about it in baseball." Rickey also said: "It is not the honor that you take with you, but the heritage you leave behind, that matters." And: "Ethnic prejudice has no place in sports, and baseball must recognize that truth if it is to maintain stature as a national game."

I take from all of these observations that Rickey knew full well that integrating the major leagues with a single man was only a stepping-stone to progress in combating racism *across America*, and that that possibility, not one man's career advancement, was actually what he was creating in his fateful discussion with Robinson.

What about Robinson? Although most people are aware of his extraordinary prowess as an athlete, few know about his history of civil rights work, which was, after his athletic accomplishments, probably the most remarkable thing about him as he sat down for that fateful meeting with Rickey in 1946. While in the Army, Robinson and boxing legend Joe Louis had joined forces to lobby the military bureaucracy to approve their applications to Officer Candidate School; they succeeded and thereby paved the way for countless other Black servicemen to join that program. Then, in 1944—a decade before Rosa Parks made headlines in Alabama for the same act of civil disobedience—Robinson refused to move to the back of a military bus when ordered to do so. He was court-martialed, but eventually acquitted, in a landmark case.

Let me mention here, too, the salient facts that both men considered themselves devout Christians and that both men saw their potential baseball alliance as a fulfillment of their spiritual calling. Their actions aligned with their stated beliefs!

There came a point during that historic conversation at Rickey's Ebbets Field office when the Brooklyn general manager insisted forcefully that he was looking for a ballplayer with the courage *not* to fight back—a requirement that gave Robinson, a proud, competitive, and deeply self-sufficient man, pause. Rickey, who had done his homework, knew that Robinson had a long history of challenging authority figures he considered racist. According to one source, Rickey looked Robinson in the eye at this point in the discussion and said: "Jackie, we've got no army. There's virtually nobody on our side. No owners, no umpires, very few newspapermen. And I'm afraid that many fans will be hostile. We'll be in a tough position. We can win only if we can convince the world that I'm doing this because you're a great ball-player, a fine gentleman." He then asked Robinson to agree not to fight back when abused...for (three) years. This request pushed Robinson well beyond his comfort zone.

Mentors know when to push you beyond your comfort zone.

After a long moment of thought, Jackie Robinson agreed to turn the other cheek. For three years. He promised Rickey that there would be no incidents. He kept that promise, not for himself, but for the country and for countless people, some of whom had not yet been born, who deserved better than hatred and racism.

These men were out to *create an environment where African Americans could be seen as the equals of other Americans—where they could compete fairly, be judged on their abilities, and be rewarded for their accomplishments.* In Steve Jobs's famous phrase, they were out to make a ding in the universe. An end to officially sanctioned racial prejudice was the Experience they were stepping into. And they were willing to literally risk their lives to make it happen.

Rickey and Robinson both knew full well that they would receive death threats by embarking together on the path that they were committing to. (Indeed, both did receive hundreds of such threats.) They knew that it took only one violent racist lunatic to end one or both of their lives. And they each decided to create the future they envisioned anyway. *They chose and created that future for others, not for themselves, not for any short-term gain, but out of a long-term purpose, one based upon the shared values of faith, equity, and justice.*

> Create a future that benefits others, not just yourself.

MALALA'S MOMENT OF TRUTH

After writing the section you just read, I challenged myself to think of a true story that exceeded the impact of Jackie Robinson's, a story about someone who had shown even deeper courage when it came to moving out of their comfort zone and taking decisive action when face to face with a Moment of Truth.

It took a while, but I did find such a story: the remarkable life's journey of a young woman from Pakistan you may have heard of—Malala Yousafzai. Often simply referred to as Malala, she is an internationally renowned activist and the youngest recipient of the Nobel Prize in the long history of that award. She received it when she was just seventeen. (She was also nominated for the International Children's Peace Prize when she was thirteen years old.)

Malala is an accomplished writer, so I will let her speak for herself.

> I was born in Mingora, Pakistan on July 12, 1997. Welcoming a baby girl is not always cause for celebration in Pakistan — but my father, Ziauddin Yousafzai, was determined to give me every opportunity a boy would have.
>
> My father was a teacher and ran a girls' school in our village. I loved school. But everything changed when the Taliban took control of our town in Swat Valley. The extremists banned many things — like owning a

television and playing music — and enforced harsh punishments for those who defied their orders. And they said girls could no longer go to school.

I spoke out publicly on behalf of girls and our right to learn. And this made me a target.

In October 2012, on my way home from school, a masked gunman boarded my school bus and asked, "Who is Malala?" He shot me on the left side of my head.

I woke up 10 days later in a hospital in Birmingham, England. The doctors and nurses told me about the attack — and that people around the world were praying for my recovery.

After months of surgeries and rehabilitation, I joined my family in our new home in the U.K. It was then I knew I had a choice: I could live a quiet life or I could make the most of this new life I had been given. I determined to continue my fight until every girl could go to school.

With my father, who has always been my ally and inspiration, I established Malala Fund, a charity dedicated to giving every girl an opportunity to achieve a future she chooses. In recognition of our work, I received the Nobel Peace Prize in December 2014 and became the youngest-ever Nobel laureate.[2]

That, I believe, is the textbook example of what an accountable response to a Moment of Truth looks like. Faced with the choice of "living a quiet life" following a near-fatal assault or creating an

---

2. "Malala's Story," *Malala.org*, Malala Fund, accessed April 21, 2021, https://malala .org/malalas-story.

Experience to step into, Malala chose the latter. She founded Malala Fund (visit them at malala.org) and began working toward the following Experience:

MALALA FUND IS WORKING FOR A WORLD WHERE EVERY GIRL CAN LEARN AND LEAD.

That powerful organizational purpose clearly dovetails with Malala's own purpose: *I determined to continue my fight until every girl could go to school.* To date, Malala Fund has raised and invested over $22 million in education initiatives for girls.

There is a lot to understand when it comes to purpose. For now, just understand that when I say purpose, I mean that which inspires you to have an impact you may not have believed was even possible. You do not have to change history, the way Jackie Robinson did. You do not have to inspire millions of people and raise millions of dollars, the way Malala has. You do not have to launch a great political career, the way John F. Kennedy did. All you have to do is accept that when you think of what is possible, you may not be seeing everything yet. When you think of what is possible in the light of your purpose and start on that journey, the magnitude of your impact will be revealed over time. With a clear sense of your unique purpose and a mentor to help keep you on track, you can become accountable, just like they were, to the commitment to pursue a higher calling.

In this chapter, you have seen three mentors at work: Joseph Kennedy Sr., Branch Rickey, and Ziauddin Yousafzai, Malala's father. Take a moment now to consider the massive impact those three gentlemen had on the world through the people they chose to mentor...and then think of someone you admire who might be able to serve as a mentor for you. No matter what stage of life you are at, you can still benefit from a mentor.

We all need someone who will speak truth into our life. We all need someone who will help us to identify and fulfill the Experience we are capable of creating. We all need someone who will help us to see and step into that Experience and set and meet the standards that will make it a reality in our lives. We all need someone who will advocate on behalf of our true potential…especially when we are not yet clear on what that potential looks like. To create the biggest and best possible future and Experience for us to step into, we all need a mentor.

MENTORSHIP: THE ORGANIZATIONAL ADVANTAGE

What I have just shared with you has powerful organizational implications, and it is not just for people with titles like "manager" and "vice president." It is for everyone! Where there is a strong organizational culture of mentorship, in my experience, there is a strong culture of accountability.

> Where there is a strong organizational culture of mentorship, there is a strong culture of accountability.

If we are playing any role in an organization—and I do mean *any* role—it is extremely important that we look for people we can mentor to help them grow. As they grow, everyone around them—including us—will grow, and the organization will develop a major competitive advantage.

Look again at the example of Branch Rickey and Jackie Robinson. Remember that Rickey had a job to do and an organization to lead. He was the general manager of the Brooklyn Dodgers. In that role, Rickey made a hiring decision that we now regard as historic. It is right that we should remember the historical impact of that hire. We should not lose sight of the fact, though, that at the time, the chief reason Rickey made that hire was that he believed it to be in the best interests of his team. Once he made that hire, Rickey made a powerful mentorship commitment, one that Robinson would speak of with deep gratitude for the rest of his life. Rickey was fully *invested* in the Experience of Robinson's success. Together, they made that Experience a reality. And they not only delivered a competitive advantage to their team (because Brooklyn won the pennant in 1947), but they set a new standard for baseball and the nation—and transformed their industry! In later years, Robinson himself served as a mentor for countless others, notably the Hall of Fame pitcher Sandy Koufax. This is the organizational power of mentorship.

Chapter Four

The Future Begins Right Now

"The future depends on what we do in the present." —Mahatma Gandhi

LOTS OF PEOPLE HEAR the word *future* and think of it as something far distant, something that is years, decades, or even centuries away. That is a major misconception. Our future begins right here and right now. It is emerging at this instant, waiting for us to shape it, and it is determined, not by outside events, but by what we decide to *lean into* in this brand-new moment as it emerges.

> Your future is emerging at this instant.

We can, like Robinson, create a compelling picture of the future we want to live, and then we can step into it. But the reverse is also true: we can create a compelling picture of a future of what frightens, annoys, or disempowers us, and we can let that picture determine the direction of our future—and our whole life. It is entirely up to us. The challenge is, we usually do this picture-making unconsciously. We do not always realize what we are doing when we make the choice to create and pursue a future that does not really support us. We do not always realize that the choice that creates the future is *ours*. But it is. We are in the driver's seat. We are always in moment-by-moment control of the future we step into, no matter what the external circumstances are and no matter what other people may be saying or doing.

The word we need to bear in mind here is *control*. We are always in full control of the decisions we make. We can either make decisions that place our focus on the influence of other people or events we cannot control...or we can make decisions that create the future *we* decide to live. If we allow other people or outside events to determine our future for us, we are choosing to relinquish control over our life. And that is never the right choice.

> It will likely take time and practice to learn to set your own course, to learn to take personal control of your future.

If you are like most people, you have some areas of your life where you may have grown used to justifying inaction by thinking (or saying), "I can't make a difference; I don't have any control in this situation." That is called the path of least resistance. And it is the opposite of accountability, for the simple reason that it is rooted in a decision to give power to that which you do not control.

Accountable people take the opposite approach. They focus on what they can control by asking themselves questions like:

- "Is this how I want to think?"

- "Is this how I want my personal relationships to be?"

- "Is this how I want to be of service to others?"

- "Is this the influence that I personally want to have on other people?"

- "Is this the impact I want my team/organization to have?"

- "Is this the world I want to live in?"

When the answer is NO, accountable people set a different mental image of the future…and then find a way to take action on that vision! Answering these questions in a way that motivates you to take *immediate* action to create a compelling future is much easier once you have identified your purpose in life and created a mission that reflects that purpose in action.

But first, we have to be honest with ourselves about something important: we are likely to need outside help in breaking the old habits and assumptions that have conditioned us to choose the path of least resistance. As we saw in the previous chapter, we are very likely to need a mentor—someone who can help us to clarify what we are doing, why we are doing it, and what is possible in our lives. Because all too often, we do not, on our own, come close to realizing what is truly possible in our lives!

LEAN INTO THE FUTURE

The best example I can give you about how this all-important process of creating the future really works comes from a sport I love: downhill skiing.

Now, downhill skiing can be a scary undertaking the first time you do it. In fact, one of the scariest moments I can recall is the time, years ago, when my ski instructor, Andy (my skiing mentor), told me that it was time to start making my way down what looked to me like a hill that was too steep for me. Just looking at the run ahead caused all kinds of adrenaline to course through my body. Mind you, the hill in question was not steep to *Andy*. I had seen him navigate it, showing me how it was done. Everything seemed effortless to Andy. But the hill he was pointing me toward certainly seemed steep to me at the time. I took a deep breath and started to move toward the edge of the downward incline.

"Hold it," Andy said. He put his hand out and stopped me. There was something in the way I approached the hill that he did not like.

"What?" I asked.

"You're leaning the wrong way. You're leaning back away from the hill. You need to lean out into it."

"Lean into it? What are you talking about? Isn't that like leaning into a punch in the boxing ring? Why on earth would I want to lean out into a steep hill? I'll lose control and fall!"

"When you lean back, your weight is not over your skis, and you can't control your movements. You want your body perpendicular to your skis so that your weight is over the middle of your skis. That way, you can control where you're going. You control the edges. You can turn if you want to turn. You can slow down if you want to slow down. You can't do any of those things if you're leaning away from the hill. When you lean in the opposite direction of the hill, you may think you're safer, but you're not, because your weight is on the back of your skis, not in the middle. All that's going to happen is you're going to lose control, your skis are going to shoot out from underneath you, and you're either going to ski off the side of the course into a tree or you're going to find yourself in the middle of a giant snowball at the bottom of the hill. Got it?"

"I think so," I said, trying hard to convince myself that my safety actually depended on doing the exact opposite of what my instinct was telling me to do.

"Just remember this," Andy said, "the steeper the hill you are heading down, the more you lean into it. While that may seem counterintuitive, that's the *only* way to survive a steep incline—by leaning into it and making sure you stay in control."

> The steeper the hill you are heading down, the more you lean into it. While that may seem counterintuitive, that's the only way to survive a steep incline—by leaning into it and making sure you stay in control.

And that's exactly what Andy taught me how to do: lean into the incline and stay in control.

Here is why I share that story with you. What happens to a beginning skier on the ski slope is *exactly* like what happens to someone who is learning to set the Experience.

We each have a choice about what kind of future we want to create for ourselves and the larger world.

> We each have a choice about the kind of future we want to create for ourselves and the larger world.

We can choose between something that is familiar and comfortable and something that is a bit of a stretch. Many times, the right course of action is counterintuitive to what we already know and expect. That is because we have not yet experienced what we are capable of. The future we could create for ourselves, the future that is a bit of a stretch, is like that hill we approach for the first time on our skis. We see a big drop coming up, and we think, *I cannot do this.* And we lean back. We do not lean into the future. Why not? Because we do not yet realize what we are capable of. But here is the problem: in leaning back, *we give up control over our lives.*

Believe me, I do realize—from direct personal experience—that what Andy was asking me to do, what I am asking you to do in this book, is counterintuitive. When we are moving forward and we see a big hill coming up, it feels wrong, at first, to lean into the incline. *But if we do not lean into it, we are never going to achieve what we're capable of achieving, and we may end up hurting ourselves or someone else.* So we need to *learn* to lean into it. And learning that is what this part of the book is all about.

The only way we can determine our true potential, the only way we can reach the level of mastery that allows us to do something effortlessly that we once thought was impossible, is to lean *into* the future we are capable of creating. And sometimes we need the help of a mentor to do that—just like I needed Andy's help in leaning into the future of being able to ski down that hill like a pro!

So for this part of the book, I want you to think of me as one of your mentors—your accountability Andy—and I want to encourage you to start leaning into a future that your first instinct might be to tense up and lean away from.

What is an important objective in your life that up to this point, you have leaned away from...but you know in your heart you could be leaning into? Is it to get out of debt? Build a truly world-class organization, one that serves and improves the lives of both customers and employees? Reach your optimal weight? Reconnect with a relative with whom you have slipped out of touch? For most of us, there is something that falls into this category. Once you have identified it, ask yourself: *How much is maintaining the status quo in this area costing me?*

Chapter Five

The Moment of Truth Is the Moment You Move Beyond What Is Comfortable

"Growth and comfort do not coexist."
—Ginni Rometty

IF YOU ARE TRULY ACCOUNTABLE, if you are consciously creating the optimal future you intend to begin living right here and right now, what you think you are capable of expands *beyond* what you are already comfortable with. If you decide never to go beyond your comfort zone, you will not be creating a compelling future. You will be creating some variation of the past.

Sadly, all too often this is what happens to both people and organizations. At the individual level, staying within your comfort zone might be deciding that it is really not worth the effort to pursue a diet and exercise routine that will get you to your ideal weight. What is the Experience you want to create in terms of physical health? What would that look and feel like? At the organizational level, staying within the comfort zone often takes the form of assuming (without any evidence) that team members are engaged with the company's mission and eager to connect and communicate with each other about how best to pursue that mission. What is the Experience you want to create in terms of employee engagement? What would that look and feel like?

There is a saying: we don't know what we don't know. That saying is absolutely correct! And it is because we don't know what we don't know that we may need someone to give us a push. I have been fortunate enough to have people in my life who pushed me beyond what I thought I was capable of—and I am a pretty driven person. I have been in numerous situations where someone I was close to—usually an advisor, a mentor, or an accountability partner—challenged me by asking, in so many words, "Sam, why are you playing it safe?" That is a question that every human being eventually needs to come to terms with, and it is almost always one that needs to be posed by someone who knows us well enough to know when it is time to give us a little encouragement when we are not pushing ourselves hard enough or fast enough in the direction we need to go.

It is easier to attain goals if we set them low. And yes, there is something to be said for making a goal realistic. Attainability is a big part of what allows us to feel and experience success. But there is also something to be said for reaching your full potential in life…and that is something we will never, ever do if we make a habit of following the path of least resistance and sticking with what is comfortable to us.

> **We will never reach our full potential by following the path of least resistance.**

MEET CARR, HIGHFILL, AND HUTCHBY

During the winter of 1984, two homeless men froze to death out on the streets of Raleigh, North Carolina. If you do not live there, you might imagine that North Carolina never gets all that cold during the winter months, but you would be wrong. Every once in a while, a winter storm gets intense and puts anyone unlucky enough to be without shelter in real danger. Three men—Paul Carr, Larry Highfill, and Jim Hutchby—read the news reports of that horrible event in 1984...and decided that they had to take action.

They realized there was a dangerous shortage of housing for the homeless in their city, and they started to take action on the future they envisioned—a future where you did not have to risk your safety, or your life, if you were down on your luck and did not have a place to stay. Carr, Highfill, and Hutchby began working hard to make that future a reality, creating resources and shelter opportunities for Raleigh's homeless community. In 1986, the three came across a large, rundown rooming house in downtown Raleigh that had gone on the market. By the spring of 1987, they had transformed that property into a transitional residence for "low-income men struggling to put their lives back together." They called the new residence Emmaus House, after the Biblical story of two followers of Jesus who encounter him on the road to Emmaus and recognize him only after they have invited him to eat with them.

When those three men read that news story, it had a special kind of impact on them. It challenged them to live up to what they said they believed. It spotlighted something in their world that needed to change, dramatically, in a positive way, starting immediately. It made them eager to create (not wait for) a future that was radically different from the world they encountered. That news story touched on who they were *as human beings*, and it inspired them to move beyond what

THE THEORY OF ACCOUNTABILITY

was comfortable or familiar to them. It inspired them to *make a decision* to create a whole different reality.

> The Moment of Truth is the moment you choose to move beyond what is comfortable to create a whole different reality, a whole different future.

THE FUTURE BEGINS WITH A DECISION

This is where creating the Experience always begins—with a decision.

Carr, Highfill, and Hutchby *decided* to take on a project that was way, way beyond what they had accomplished and experienced before. That took courage, it took self-awareness, and it took a conversation involving more than one person. Creating the Experience always requires a conversation with someone else!

Think of the most important accomplishments in your life, the decisions and actions you are proudest of. Are you thinking of one right now? Good. Now ask yourself: Did it involve other people?

Of course it did. No matter what that moment was, I guarantee you that if you are truly proud of it, it involved some kind of interaction, at some point, with another human being. You talked to someone about your plans. Or you were moved by someone else's experience and decided to take action. Or you learned something from someone you respected. Or you had a conversation with someone and realized that the two of you were meant to work on a certain undertaking—together. Or all of the above!

As you consider the Experience you are moved to create, be on the lookout for allies and mentors. Remember that we build our most important relationships with people who have values that align with our values. There is power in the conversations we have with such people. We come to understand that they think through challenges in the same way we do...and we inspire and support each other over time as we bring the Experience to life. It is through those special relationships, those special conversations, that truly great things happen.

> Creating the Experience requires a conversation with someone else. If you have not talked about the future you are creating with another human being, you are not creating the Experience.

Eventually, the courageous decision of these three men to envision and create more and better options for the homeless in their community led to the creation of a powerful vision for what life should be like in Raleigh for people facing major challenges: *all people have a safe place to recover.* The three friends also created a mission to match that vision: *to provide safe, affordable, recovery housing within a supportive community.*

Today, you can find that vision and that mission on their website. You can also visit Emmaus House for yourself, and you can see for yourself the difference it has made in the lives of people in the community. But when you look at what their years of work accomplished—when you look at the end result of any powerful Experience that some accountable person has set—do not imagine that it came about by magic. It all started with a *decision*.

There is a special kind of power that arises from believing something so deeply that you can step right into the reality that aligns with that belief and choose to make it your future, starting immediately.

When you make the most powerful decisions, you are creating an Experience that aligns with your very best self, based on your deepest understanding of who you are as a person and what you are here on earth to do. You are putting a stake in the ground and saying, "This is the future I am choosing to create, in this moment, because this is who I am." These decisions are where the power is. When you make such a decision, you are not being compelled to take action by someone else; you are taking the steering wheel of your own life in both hands and choosing exactly where to go next, based on your own conviction about the direction you are meant to take in life.

Nothing changes for the better in our lives until we make a decision about the kind of Experience we want to create. Once we decide to take action in a certain direction that supports who we know ourselves to be, we are cutting ourselves off from countless other options. The things we are deciding *not* to do may be more comfortable, more known, more familiar to us—but in making a decision about the Experience we want, we are making the conscious choice to let go of that comfort and expand what is possible for ourselves and others by saying YES to a new direction, a new trajectory, a new possibility in life. Everything starts happening once you make this kind of decision!

> The Moment of Truth is a powerful moment. It always propels us forward, toward a decision that creates a newer and fuller expression of the person we are meant to be.

Many people struggle with making accountable decisions. They avoid decisions that take them beyond what is comfortable to them. They do not set and create a future consciously, based on the kind of person they are meant to be. They follow the path of least resistance. *We do not want to follow their example, no matter how tempting it may be to do so.* We cannot be truly accountable by doing what everyone else is doing!

Once we make a conscious decision to set the future we want to create, once we choose not to follow the path of least resistance, not to play it safe, *we are in the minority.* How many people came across that same news story that Carr, Highfill, and Hutchby read and never took any kind of action on it? Thousands. Tens of thousands, probably. But what I want you to notice is that they had a very different kind of response. For them, reading that story was a Moment of Truth—because it caused them to go beyond their comfort zone.

We all face our own Moments of Truth, moments when we are challenged to make an accountable decision that sets the Experience and creates a compelling future. That future always has three critical components.

- *The future you decide to create has to be non-negotiable.* Changing the status quo for the homeless community in Raleigh was not something Carr, Highfill, and Hutchby *wanted* to do, *hoped* to do, or *planned to get around* to doing. It was something that was happening from the moment they took it on, and it was not up for debate.

- *The future you choose to create has to matter deeply to you on a personal level.* The mission the three friends undertook was integral to who they were as human beings because it connected to their deepest sense of purpose, their sense of what they were truly meant to do in life, and it led to the creation of a mission that was that purpose in action.

- *Last but certainly not least, the future you choose to create has to be something you discuss with people who are important to you.* Discussing your Moment of Truth with others makes it more likely that people will engage with you about that future. These discussions not only enlist support, but they also cause the resources you need to flow in your direction.

> The future you choose to create has to be connected to your very best self. We become our best selves only when we allow someone to help us—and when we are helping someone else to become their best self.

Chapter Six

Excuse or Possibility?

"Never make excuses. Your friends don't need them and your foes won't believe them." —John Wooden

EACH OF US FACES Moments of Truth in life, moments when we are called upon to make a decision that supports our best conception of ourselves…even though it might seem easier, more convenient, more familiar, and more comfortable to stick with the status quo. These are moments when we are challenged to remember, and act on, our own understanding of who we are truly meant to be. The decisions we make in these Moments of Truth define us as human beings.

Sometimes the choices we make during a Moment of Truth *are* rooted in excuses: we often make such a decision based on a limited understanding of what we believe ourselves to be capable of, based on our own past experience. For instance, a relative makes a demeaning joke that we do not find funny, a joke comes at the expense of an entire group of people. We know that laughing at that joke violates our values, and at some level we also know that what we allow in our space, we condone.

What we allow in our space, we condone.

But we laugh at the joke anyway and change the subject, perhaps because we do not feel like speaking up or we believe people will think less of us if we find a sensitive, tactful way to say what we feel. In those moments, we take what we have done in the past—laugh politely and change the subject—as the pattern for the future we choose to create. We do not grow and develop as individuals. We also do not help others to grow and be better, and we do not create a better place for everyone to coexist.

At other times, the choices we make at such moments are based on *possibility*. If we are fortunate, they are reinforced by others in our circle who help us to focus on what we *could be* capable of, as opposed to what we *have been* capable of. And we decide to push beyond our comfort zone. Perhaps we say something like, "Uncle Jim, I realize that I probably should have said something about this a long time ago, and I am sincerely sorry that I didn't, but I really think we can find something better to joke about. That kind of joke makes me uncomfortable, and I know that's not what you want to do. Have you heard the one about...." And we might just be surprised by how others who hear that kind of thing will step up and support us.

When we respond in *that* way to a Moment of Truth, our decisions go beyond what once seemed possible. Our decisions begin to create a future based on possibility, and they carry a positive impact on ourselves and others. That impact may affect us and others for a few minutes, a few days, a whole lifetime, or even longer—but we are never the same, having made that decision and created a different future.

Let me take a moment to share with you what led up to one of the big Moments of Truth in my life—a decision moment that had a profound effect on me and many other people.

MY MOMENT OF TRUTH

This was 2012. I had recently been introduced to a remarkable gentleman named J. Pat Hickman, who at that time was the president, CEO, and chairman of the board of a bank based in Amarillo, Texas, called Happy State Bank. The bank had earned a reputation for superior service, an extraordinary working culture, and *expanding its market share and improving its bottom line* during the financial crisis of 2008–2009. As you may recall, that global crisis hit the banking and financial services sector very hard.

Happy State Bank's mission statement made me smile every time I read it:

Work hard, have fun, make money, while providing outstanding customer service and honoring the Golden Rule.

I set an appointment with Pat so we could get to know each other a little better and find out whether it might make sense to work together. My assistant Sharon Miner, who had introduced me to Pat, came with me to that meeting.

Pat was a big fan of my work. He loved my book *No More Excuses*. And I could tell he was excited by what I had to say about accountability. About thirty minutes into that conversation with him in his office, he jumped up, went over to his computer, turned it on, and printed out four sheets of paper. He came back to where we were sitting, handed them to me, and said, "Sam, I want you to know what I believe and what we believe here at Happy State Bank."

I said, "Okay."

"There are a lot of people," he went on, warming to his topic, "who feel that there ought to be a book about this little bank."

In that moment, before I had even begun to read the sheets he had handed me, I was thinking, "Hmm. A book about a bank. Is that really the kind of thing that would keep me up at night, turning pages?" I was pretty sure the answer was NO. Think of this from my perspective. I was a published author, and I liked to think I had a decent sense of what the market was looking for. I was pretty sure this was not it. After all, there are only two things you can do at a bank: put money in and take money out. Why would someone want to read a book about a little bank in Amarillo, Texas?

As those thoughts were going through my mind, Pat went on: "A lot of people have asked to write about our bank. I've never come across anyone I felt was right for this project. But I really loved your book *No More Excuses*. I think you might just be the person to write this book."

Something about his tone of voice made me stop and reconsider what he was suggesting. What if I could turn this into the kind of project where the bank would agree to buy a large number of books up front as promotional resources and put a lot of money into marketing and promoting the book? I started to see dollar signs. Maybe this would make sense after all. In the moment, I did not realize how powerful those four pages really were. I did not fully grasp what had been handed to me and the power it contained. I was focused on the wrong thing: the money. I was not in a mindset of abundance; I was in a scarcity mindset. It was only later that those four pages became critically important to me. At the time, my thinking was purely transactional. I wanted to close the deal. And because of that I almost lost the entire opportunity.

I told myself that the money was more important than the chance to build this relationship. That was an excuse. An excuse is a story you tell yourself to sell yourself and try to sell to others.

> An excuse is a story you tell yourself to sell yourself and try to sell to others.

A couple of weeks later, I sent Pat a proposal for a major book project, encompassing not just the creation of the book, but a full-scale promotional initiative I had designed to turn the book we would create into a big success. Pat took a look at it and told me frankly that he could not pass it along to his board because he did not believe they would make the investment. He did not see the same value that I was seeing. Life went on. We stayed in touch. I kept reading and rereading those four sheets of paper he had printed out for me in his office. They outlined a way of working, a way of *thinking*, that really stuck with me. I kept talking about them with the people in my life and about Happy State Bank's remarkable story.

Several months went by. I could not manage to resuscitate the deal. A day came when I was on the phone with my assistant, Sharon Miner. Sharon was one of the people with whom I had been talking, not just excitedly, but with a sense of growing purpose, about those four pages Pat had given me.

At a certain point in the call I said to Sharon, "I really wish we could have gotten together with Happy State Bank and written that book. I think it would have been a great project. He just doesn't get the book business I guess. I guess it just wasn't a good fit. If the dollars aren't there, why should it be me to tell that story?"

There was a long silence on the line.

"I'll tell you why it should be you, Sam," she said. "I watched you when Pat talked at that leadership event in Amarillo. I watched you at the business roundtable you both attended. And I watched you during the meeting we had with Pat at the bank. Something about you changes when Pat's in the room. You think about what is possible in a different way. You have a different way of looking at your own purpose. He's got an important story to tell. And you need to hear it, too. I am telling you, Sam, if you walk away from this project, you will regret it. And if you ask me, you were born to do this book."

It was like she had stepped through the phone and looked me straight in the eyes. I realized Sharon was right. I had a choice to make: follow through on something that I believed in my heart that I was meant to do, or ignore it. Ignoring it meant buying into another excuse. And I was no longer willing to do that.

From that moment on, it was clear to me: I was there to write that book, not to come up with a fancy proposal, not to set up a marketing campaign—*to write the book.* That was what I was meant to do. There was a powerful feeling of certainty coursing through me as I said to Sharon, "Pat has spoken on several occasions of providence in his life. If providence is present in Pat's life, and if it brought the two of us together, then it must be present in my life, too." I knew the door was open and I needed to walk through it. I just needed to say, "Yes."

"You're right, Sharon," I said. "I gotta run. Bye."

I had practically hung up on Sharon. It was clear what I needed to do and I did not want to waste a minute. I called Pat and asked him, "Are you still interested in me writing that book?"

He responded, "Yes, I am."

"Well, we are going to find a way to do this. Forget the agreement. Forget the cost. I'll write the book. We'll figure out who will publish it and how all the pieces go together as we proceed." And that's exactly what we did.

That book, *Non-Negotiable,* not only transformed my business, it transformed my life. It launched a brand-new book contract with a new publisher. It touched people all over the world and motivated them to make radical, positive changes in their lives and organizations. It put all the work I had done up to that point in my career into focus, and it allowed me to sharpen and hone my message in a way that made it more powerful, compelling, and accessible to other people than it had ever been before. *Non-Negotiable* led me to countless new business opportunities, and it enabled me to create entirely new programs and help thousands of people with whom I would never have otherwise connected. And nearly a decade later, it is still showing up on Amazon's bestseller lists. Oh, and those four sheets of paper Pat shared came to mean a great deal to me. They described the core values of Happy State Bank and Trust, and they had a huge impact on me, my business, and my clients, because they laid the groundwork for my ability to help organizations around the world to discover, establish, and sustain their own powerful narratives about organizational values.[3]

The point is, with Sharon's help, I recognized a Moment of Truth for what it was, and I responded appropriately to it by making a purposeful decision—a decision that aligned with who I really am as a person. Once I made that decision, things started to fall into place. I began to recognize new opportunities, change my mindset to one of abundance, and take action. The bounty that followed was immeasurable.

And it all came about because I recognized, and acted on, a Moment of Truth!

> **Each of us faces Moments of Truth that are unique to us.**

What emerges as a Moment of Truth to me may not be a Moment of Truth for you. The way I respond to my Moment of Truth may be

---

3.   To learn more about Happy State Bank's core values, see my book *Non-Negotiable*.

totally different from the way you respond to yours. Our job is never to tell someone else what their Moment of Truth is or how they should respond to it. Our job is simply to recognize these moments and then to make the right decision, a decision based on the possibility of fulfilling our own purpose as human beings.

Notice that I am talking about your purpose in a deeply personal sense here, the kind of calling that may take a lifetime to refine fully. There is still a lot to learn about what this means, I know. But for now, just consider that making a truly purposeful decision—the kind of decision Carr, Highfill, and Hutchby made when they came across that newspaper story, the kind that Jackie Robinson made when challenged by Branch Rickey to go outside of his comfort zone and look beyond the abuse he would receive in the big leagues—is how we create the future. It is how we awaken our very best selves. It is creating the Experience. It is recognizing the Moment of Truth and then choosing a path that opens up a new possibility, a path that supports our best understanding of who we are and what we are meant to accomplish in life. Whether or not we have walked down it before, creating the Experience means taking the next step on the path called *Who I Am Supposed to Be.*

> **Making a purposeful decision is how we create the future.**

"Take the first step in faith. You don't have to see the whole staircase, just take the first step." —Martin Luther King, Jr.

Chapter Seven

Purpose and Experience

CREATING THE EXPERIENCE means embracing our unique purpose and then stepping into the future that matches up with that purpose…even when that purpose points us toward a future we do not yet believe we are capable of creating.

> Creating the Experience means embracing our purpose and then stepping into the future that matches up with that purpose… even when that purpose points us toward a future we do not yet believe we are capable of creating.

If you do not yet know what your purpose is and are having trouble connecting it to the Experience you want to create, relax. You have plenty of company! This is where most people find themselves in life… but it is not where you have to stay. Let's talk for a moment about how to identify your purpose, because creating the Experience is impossible if you have not yet gained at least some personal clarity on this.

Identifying our purpose is a difficult business only if we choose to make it difficult. We often do make it difficult, though, by expecting our purpose to line up, forever, with a couple of words we have picked more or less at random. Actually, our purpose becomes clearer to us over time. It is only natural that the words we use to express that purpose should shift a little bit as we gain deeper and deeper certainty about, and comfort with, who we are and what we are here for.

Even so, our purpose is always waiting for us. It speaks to us and becomes more obvious to us in Moments of Truth.

> **Our purpose speaks to us and becomes more obvious in Moments of Truth.**

Our job is to recognize our purpose in those moments, to take action on our purpose whenever the opportunity arises, to learn to create new opportunities to take action on our purpose, and to do our best to put our purpose into words concisely and accurately so that we can remind ourselves of it regularly.

How will we recognize our purpose? There are four important signals:

- *The purpose brings us a sense of personal fulfillment whenever we pursue it.* This feeling of fulfillment (some call it joy) is evident immediately. When you are doing what you are meant to be doing, you feel a special kind of deep personal happiness that you do not get anywhere else.

- *The purpose connects to serving others.* We are all connected! Which means our purpose must connect to serving others. This connection to other people may *not* be immediately obvious. It may only emerge over time, or indirectly. For instance, becoming the best painter you can possibly become is, at least at first, a matter of reaching your own potential and achieving the best and highest work of which you, personally, are capable in the field of painting. Does pursuing that purpose by picking up a paintbrush serve another person? Maybe not at first. But the act of becoming the best painter you are capable of being means you are growing and developing as a person, and that arc of personal growth is going to make it easier for you to identify and act on opportunities that come your way to help and support other people in your life. Eventually, the quest for self-improvement has to connect, directly or indirectly, to helping someone *else*. If an activity or aspiration benefits *only* you and never has even an indirect positive impact on anyone else, it is not what I call a purposeful aspiration. By the same token, an activity or aspiration that disregards the rights of others is not purposeful.

- *The purpose inspires us to move beyond what we have done before.* The purpose makes us eager to do more, be more, become more…because it lies at the heart of our life. The more clearly we understand it, the more often our purpose motivates us to take action that points us toward some new level of achievement or contribution. Not only that—we become excited, animated, and engaged whenever we communicate about our purpose with others, and that enthusiasm impacts others positively.

- *Taking action on our purpose gives us a clearer sense of who we are meant to be.* Whether we succeed or fail in the short term in pursuing an objective that connects to our purpose, the action itself confirms a powerful internal sense that we are going where we need to go in life. Note that your purpose may connect to a mission that extends beyond the borders of your own lifetime! Make a list of the historical figures you admire most, and I suspect you will notice that the people on that list intentionally made this kind of commitment. Think of Lincoln, or Gandhi, or Mother Teresa. Did the reality that they did not live to see the fullest expression of their positive impact on the human race detract from their legacy—or add to it? *Create an Experience that will outlive you!*

Create an Experience that will outlive you!

Once you know what your purpose is, you can clarify the mission to which it connects. Your mission is your purpose in action. Once you are clear on the mission, you can talk about it and engage people in it! This is incredibly important. As soon as we verbalize the mission, it becomes a commitment, and we align with it in a very powerful, personal way. Not only that—when we announce our mission to the people in our world, we give them an opportunity to come on board and be a part of that mission! *But you must know your purpose before you start talking about your mission!*

Your mission is your purpose in action.

It is a good idea, at least once a year, to set aside a few hours to explore your purpose and determine whether you need to refine the words you use to describe it.

> Our unique purpose is the service at the heart of our life that inspires us, fulfills us, and clarifies who we are meant to be.

By way of example, my purpose is:

To help people discover their potential and be the best they can possibly be.

It took me decades to formulate those sixteen words, and I know I may not be done redefining them yet. But they wake me up and inspire me to take action every time I come in contact with them, which is why I put them someplace I will see them, each and every day! Those sixteen words powerfully summarize the reason I am here, the big WHY in my life. Whenever I read that sentence, I wake up to my purpose.

Note that a powerful statement of purpose shines a spotlight on the big WHY in your life, without being too specific about the actions, initiatives, and beliefs that support that big WHY. You can fill in the blanks on that later with what I call a Mission Narrative. Remember, your mission is your purpose in action. It is what you DO to support your purpose. Again, for the sake of example, let me share my own Mission Narrative so you know what one looks like.

MISSION

My mission is to build a more accountable world. I serve my mission through three specific activities:

TEACH

I am a teacher. I educate people on ways to improve and be their best. I share new insights and ways of looking at

issues, challenges, and opportunities. I share different ways of believing and thinking.

INSPIRE

Through the use of events, experiences, and evidence I support the beliefs that I teach. This breathes life into the beliefs and helps people take action. I help people to awaken to their true purpose in life.

SUPPORT

I come alongside and help people take the "first step" in their new adventure. I provide ongoing encouragement, tools, and resources to help people stay on course. Change is difficult. We all face challenges throughout our journey. I stay ready to help others overcome those challenges and achieve the goals they aspire to.

My Mission Narrative makes clear that my aim of creating an accountable world connects to three specific activities: teaching, inspiring, and supporting. It goes into an appropriate amount of detail about what those words mean to me. This is important, because what I mean when I use the word "support" may not be what you mean when you use the same word!

Notice that we support our purpose by taking on a mission that is capable of inspiring others. The purpose can be kept private, but the mission (which, again, is our purpose in action) is always something we find a way to share with the rest of the world.

Purpose and mission are the tools we use to create our Experience, the future we choose to step into.

> **Purpose and mission are the tools we use to create our Experience, the future we choose to step into.**

In my case, the mission is building a more accountable world. I believe you can do that only by helping people be accountable individually. I believe you can do *that* only by building more accountable relationships. And I also believe that when you build more accountable relationships, it is easier to build accountable organizations. Once you build more accountable organizations, I believe you help to create more accountable communities. And finally, I believe that building accountability within the community in which you live leads to a more accountable world.

I am here for all of that...because building an accountable world helps people discover their potential and be the best they can possibly be.

JACKIE ROBINSON'S PURPOSE

Recall that Jackie Robinson was not playing baseball just for himself in the difficult years that followed his debut with the Brooklyn Dodgers. Recall that he had promised Branch Rickey that he would not respond in kind when abused, attacked, and demeaned, on or off the field. Recall that he kept that promise, despite enormous provocation and a long personal history of standing up for himself against racists who challenged or insulted him.

Why?

Robinson kept that promise not to make himself famous, not to fatten his bank account, but as a *service* for the whole country—indeed, for the larger world. When he confronted obstacles, some of them brutal, he stepped back and reconnected with a mission that supported his purpose, which was to *create an environment where African Americans could be seen as the equals of other Americans—where they could compete fairly, be judged on their abilities, and be rewarded for their accomplishments.* That was his mission. That was his journey.

If that meant that while Robinson was playing first base, a runner who had been raised in the South got to slice open Robinson's thigh with his spikes without Robinson being able to slug the guy—and on at least one occasion, that is exactly what Robinson's journey meant—so be it. Robinson later admitted that he very nearly fought back against that assault…but then he thought better of it. He remembered his promise to Branch Rickey.

When his teammates started making plans to retaliate against Enos Slaughter, the player who had spiked him, Robinson dissuaded them—again, in order to fulfill his purpose. He knew he could not break his promise, and he knew that any news reports about retaliation for the incident on the field would be likely to cast him in a bad light… and that that would only make things harder for the Black players he hoped would follow him into the big leagues. That, he knew, would not fulfill his purpose.

Robinson's wife Rachel spoke to this purpose when she said of her late husband, "I never once heard Jack say, out loud, 'I want to give up.' Or: 'I don't think I can take it anymore.' He would get discouraged, he'd get frustrated, he'd get angry. But by the next morning, you know, he'd kind of sleep it off, and the next day was a new day. I think he felt that he could transcend this provocation because he had a higher goal. I mean, the goal was important to him. The mission was important to him."

Chapter Eight

Take the Time

"There is no greater gift you can give or receive than to honor your calling. It's why you were born. And how you become most truly alive." —Oprah Winfrey

THERE ARE NOT GOING TO BE many points in this book where I ask you to put the book down and go do something, but we are about to have one of those moments. To get the most out of this book, to get *anything* out of this book, you will need to invest a little time to get greater clarity on your purpose in life. Why? Because without that clarity, you may miss a Moment of Truth…and you may find yourself making decisions that do not support the future you deserve.

> Invest the time necessary to get
> a clear sense of your purpose in life.

Investing the time to get a clearer sense of your purpose in life is a little like being a world-class runner, someone who is preparing to run a big race. Let's say you are a marathon runner. You know you are going to need a good pair of shoes for that twenty-six-mile race. So you go to the store that specializes in running shoes.

That is because this decision is worth getting right. It is worth making the trip. It is worth investing the time. So you take that time. You do not order the shoes online. You examine them in person and talk to someone who is an expert in running shoes. You look at all the different options, and you take a lot of different factors into account. Not just factors like color and styling, but also factors like good arch support, because you happen to have a high arch, and side support, because you overpronate—meaning your ankle rolls a little too far downward and inward with each step you take. And of course, after taking all of those questions into account, you want to try the shoe on and make sure it fits you, because you have found that very often, shoes that are marked as being the correct size for you are somehow a little too big or a little too small, and running in a shoe that does not fit you is a major barrier in an important race and can lead to pain, blisters, or both. *Any* problem with fit, repeated over the course of a twenty-six-mile run, can escalate into catastrophe.

The point is, you do not want just *any* shoe; you want the right shoe *for you* so you can run the race that you have signed up for and are now preparing to run. Picking the wrong shoe—the shoe that might be right for somebody else who is built differently—carries major dangers. Who knows what kind of trouble, pain, or injury running a marathon in the wrong pair of shoes can do to your ankles, legs, hips, or spine?

The marathon is your life. The shoe is your purpose. It *has* to be a great fit. In fact, it has to be a *perfect* fit—a fit for you and no one else. If you choose the wrong one, if you are "wearing" a purpose that you picked because you heard that it works great for someone else, but it does not work for you, then everything is going to get out of alignment. And as you run your race, the problems are going to magnify. What might have started out as a minor irritation will become a major problem. You will not only risk the outcome of the race, but you will also risk hurting yourself and others.

THIS IS YOUR MOMENT

Every decision you make—every single one—interacts with your purpose. It either supports that purpose or it does not.

> Every decision you make—every single one—interacts with your purpose. It either supports that purpose or it does not.

Right now, you face a decision. Here it is: *At the end of this chapter, will you take the time to set your purpose into words that are a perfect fit for you…or will you keep reading and tell yourself you will do this part later?*

"You may delay, but time will not, and lost time is never found again."
—Benjamin Franklin

In just a moment, I will ask you to set aside *at least half an hour* to think about your purpose and to set it into words. Make a decision *right now* to take that step when I ask you to.

First, a little guidance: You will want to use these thirty precious minutes to brainstorm your purpose in life. Make sure it is *your* purpose, no one else's. It is fine to do a lot of writing if you want to, but remember that the end result you are after is to keep your written statement of purpose brief. Aim for just a sentence or two. As you brainstorm, remember the criteria I shared with you a little earlier: your purpose gives you a sense of deep fulfillment, it connects to serving others, it inspires you to move beyond what you have done before, and it gives you a clearer sense of who you are meant to be.

I strongly recommend that you start by thinking about the concept of service. If we look closely enough for our own unique purpose, I believe we will always see that no matter how personal the purpose we discover may be to our own life and experience, it can always be found within the *service* we render to others.

Your purpose connects you to your best personal understanding of how you can serve others. Sometimes, people make the mistake of believing that the simple fact that they are good at something makes that thing their purpose. Wrong. Whatever it is they do well *must eventually connect to some kind of service* if it supports their purpose in life.

> If you believe you have found your purpose, but your purpose does not connect in any way to serving another person, keep looking!

Please put the book down now and take at least half an hour to come up with one or two written sentences, recorded in a notebook, journal, or your digital writing tool of choice, that capture your purpose. **Make the decision to do this right now!**

Chapter Nine

Living Your Purpose Means Pursuing Fulfillment, Not Happiness

"A life is not important except in the impact it has on other lives."
—Jackie Robinson

AT THIS POINT, I am going to assume that you have written at least an initial draft of a sentence or two describing a purpose that serves others, inspires you, and leaves you feeling fulfilled when you are aligned with it.

You may have noticed that when I shared the criteria for identifying your purpose, I did not ask you to make one of the conditions for your life's purpose that it makes you *happy*. Instead, I asked you to focus on whether pursuing your purpose left you feeling *fulfilled*. The distinction is an important one, and I want to spend a little time examining it here, for the simple reason that devoting yourself to *happiness* can lead you into decisions that do not point you toward the kind of future you actually want to live.

That may seem counterintuitive, but hear me out. Happiness is a construct, one that, for the most part, is created by other people.

> **Happiness is a construct, one that, for the most part, is created by other people.**

Lots of people go out of their way to convince us what our happiness should be. Friends and relatives may tell us that making the same kinds of decisions they have made in their lives, or the decisions they *wish* they had made in their lives, will make us happy. They may even tell us that making *them* happy is what will make us happy. People who are popular on social media may tell us that following their advice, or their example, will make us happy. Advertisements may tell us that buying a new pickup truck, or going on a vacation to the Bahamas, or buying the newest phone, or listening to a download of Weird Al Yankovic's greatest hits, will make us happy, and we may end up believing all of that is true. No offense intended to Weird Al, or any of those other people, but that is crazy.

I will never presume to tell you what will make you happy. I do not know what is going to make you happy, and I am not entirely sure the goal of living a happy life is realistic or even achievable.

Happiness comes and goes, and it is a deeply personal experience, something that cannot be dictated to you by anyone else. Yet all too often, people allow themselves to be convinced to look to others for how to attain or even define happiness.

We may think that we have defined happiness for ourselves, but if we examine the situation closely, I think we will usually find that it is external influences—friends, family, media, marketing professionals—that play a dominant role in setting the borders that define what "happiness" is and is not in our lives. And all too often, when we try to turn the artificial construct we call "happiness" into reality by chasing after something we have been convinced will make us happy, we end up feeling deeply disappointed and empty, *even when we obtain the thing people told us would make us happy.*

Happiness is fleeting; fulfillment endures. Happiness that endures never shows up. We find ourselves on a quest that we can never complete. We are going to have moments when we are happy and moments when we are unhappy. That is life.

> **Happiness is fleeting; fulfillment endures.**

It is *fulfillment* we should be striving for. I prefer this word because fulfillment is obviously unique to us. No one else can tell us when we are fulfilled or claim to know what will bring us fulfillment. We have to figure that out on our own. And what we inevitably find, sooner or later, is that only one thing actually leaves us feeling fulfilled: *pursuing our purpose.*

> **Sooner or later we figure out that only one thing actually leaves us feeling fulfilled: pursuing our purpose.**

If you are living your purpose, you will find fulfillment. I guarantee it.

That fulfillment will energize you. It will get you up early and keep you going late into the night. It will point you toward the right lessons, the right resources, the right people, and the right achievements. When you are connected to a purpose that inspires you, a purpose that empowers you to find the best and highest way to serve others, you will know with certainty that you are walking the path you were meant to walk in life. And knowing that will give you what you need to get through good times and bad times.

Chapter Ten

Living Your Purpose Means Creating the Future

"How wonderful it is that nobody needs to wait a single moment to start improving the world."
—Anne Frank

The word **CREATE** is powerful.

Creation is really what this whole book is about. It is the essence of the $E=mc^2$ formula I shared with you at the beginning of this book. As you read these words, you are *creating* the Experience, the E in that formula. You have within you the ability to create any future you choose to step into; there is something very special about that ability. Never forget that is what you are doing: *creating* the future, *creating* the destination of your life and the lives of those you impact, all by means of the decisions you make.

This is a sacred journey. We all have the power to use our decisions to create a future we believe is worth living, a future worth stepping into. No conscious human being is lacking in that capability. This is a gift that we have all received. It is part of being human, but not all human beings recognize that they have been given that gift. Some do not feel worthy of that gift. Some do not think it exists; they have convinced themselves that others create their future. But the gift of decision is always ours, and in using that gift consciously, in alignment with our purpose, we can always make decisions that align with our purpose, decisions that create a future based on possibility.

> **We all have the power to use our decisions to create a future that we believe is worth living.**

If, this morning, you happen to pass someone crouching on a city street corner with a little cup placed in front of him, holding a handwritten sign that reads I NEED MONEY FOR POT, *know that that person is creating a future.* To me, it is not a future based on a particularly inspiring possibility. He could be setting his sights a lot higher than he is at the moment. But make no mistake: he is building the future he is willing and able to step into. And so is everyone else.

At any given moment, we are creating the future that we are about to experience. We are doing that with our choices. The only challenge is, most of us do it without *realizing* that that is what we are doing or even without realizing that we have the power to do it.

> **At any given moment, we are creating the future that we are about to experience.**

My challenge to you is to *recognize* that you have that power and then to use it in a way that produces something that touches your life and the lives of others in a powerful, positive way, something that makes the world better. Not just better for you—better for other people. That, after all, is what service is all about.

LIVE THE FUTURE YOU DESIGN

Your future can be something you design, not something that happens by default. The future can be something you decide makes sense for yourself and others, not something you happen to be used to doing or that other people have been doing and that you decide to do because you want them to approve of you. The future you step into can be a conscious choice. You have that power.

This is the whole reason I wrote this book: I want that power to be something you are aware of and take *conscious* action on. Unconscious action is typically what is already happening. I wrote this book to help you to raise your game. The process of creating your future is already taking place. You are creating your future right now, with every decision you make, whether you realize it or not. Once you realize that your decisions and your future are within your control and you take full responsibility for that, then you get to direct where this awesome power flows. *Living with purpose means creating the future you choose, a future that has a positive impact on others.*

Chapter Eleven

Living Your Purpose Means Recognizing Excuses…and Moving Beyond Them

"Argue for your limitations and, sure enough, they're yours."

—Richard Bach

WHEN YOU ARE LIVING your purpose, you do not get stopped by excuses, those stories you tell yourself to sell yourself and try to sell to others. I am talking about stories like:

"I am too young."

"I am too old."

"I don't have enough experience."

"I should not even try, because the odds are against me."

"People won't take me seriously."

"There is no way to achieve what I want to achieve."

These kinds of stories are not just negative self-talk—they are toxic, false narratives that undercut your unique purpose and make it impossible for you to learn what you need to learn in order to become the best possible version of yourself.

The only antidote to excuses is to refocus, with intensity, on those things you can control in your life that connect to your purpose: the big Why that inspires you, gets you up early, and keeps you up late. One reliable way of refocusing on your unique purpose is to read the written words of your purpose statement multiple times a day. You can read them silently or out loud. The choice is yours. But I strongly recommend that you make reading those words an integral part of your day.

> **The only antidote to excuses is to refocus, with intensity, on those things you can control in your life that connect to your purpose.**

I call the state of mind that recognizes excuses for what they are, rejects them, reorients you toward what you need to be doing, and pulls you into a better future, being ON PURPOSE. If reading your written statement does not instantly put you ON PURPOSE, redraft the statement until it does!

When you are ON PURPOSE...

...you are engaged in activities that align with your purpose.

...you focus on that which you can control, not that which you cannot control.

...you identify new opportunities, even when you face opposition or adversity.

...you think creatively.

...you are all about service.

...you connect to something bigger than yourself.

...you inspire others.

...you are always looking for ways to make contributions to your relationships.

...you leave the drama behind.

...you set aside what isn't working and invest your time and attention in what is working.

...you look for ways to take constructive actions that build and expand the Experience you are stepping into.

...you create the future.

Even in those moments when you are not ON PURPOSE, you always have the option of changing what you are focusing on, changing what you are doing...and finding your way back to your purpose.

Chapter Twelve

Put What You Have Learned about the "E" in E=mc^2 into Practice!

"The future belongs to those who believe in the beauty of their dreams."
—Eleanor Roosevelt

NOW THAT YOU HAVE LEARNED about Experience, you are ready to take the next step. Here are some powerful questions about Experience for you to consider. The more detailed your answers, the better prepared you will be to put what you know into practice.

- What desired Experience has a Moment of Truth pointed you toward? What area of your life does that desired Experience connect to? How does that desired Experience connect to your personal sense of purpose? Whom do you serve as you create that Experience?

- What is one specific Experience you are personally driven to create? How does this desired experience connect to other aspects of your life and/or your business?

- What do you want to Experience in terms of your own health and well-being?

- What do you want your Experience of your relationships to be? *A very important follow-up question to that is:* What do each of *those* people need to experience in order for you to create that Experience?

- *If you're in a romantic relationship:* What do you want your Experience with your spouse or significant other to be? What would they have to experience in order for that to happen?

- *If you have kids:* What do you want your Experience with your children to be? What would they have to experience in order for that to happen?

- What do you want your Experience with your parents to be? What would they have to experience in order for that to happen?

- What do you want your Experience with your closest friends to be? What would they have to experience in order for that to happen?

- What do you want your Experience with your neighbors to be? What would they have to experience in order for that to happen?

- What do you want your Experience with your co-workers to be? What would they have to experience in order for that to happen?

- What Experience do you want to have with the people in your community? What would they have to experience in order for that to happen?

- If you have a leadership role in a business:

  - What do you want the Experience of your team members to be? What would they have to experience in order for that to happen?

  - What do you want your Experience with customers to be? (For instance, do you want them to come back? Do you want them to feel safe? Do you want them to recommend you to others?) What would customers have to experience in order for that to happen?

  - What Experience would you like to see from your business or your team in terms of performance outcomes (such as referrals, margin, or closed sales)? What would your team members have to experience in order for that to happen?

I realize this seems like a lot, but let me explain why I am sharing so many examples with you. We need to be *consistently* asking ourselves these kinds of questions, day after day, because once we come up with answers that align with our purpose, we are living with purpose, on purpose, and for a purpose. The answers we come up with allow us to create an Experience by *design*, not by default; an Experience shaped by our personal sense of who we are meant to be.

- So take, for instance, the question of what Experience you want in your relationship with your spouse. You might answer that you want them to experience feeling important, valued, cherished, or heard. Great. Now: How are you going to define that further? What is likely to make your spouse feel that way? And how does helping your spouse to feel that way align with your purpose?

- Or let's say you are thinking in terms of an Experience that connects to the people who report to you. Let's say you want the Experience of having the lowest employee turnover rate in your industry. Follow it out. How is that outcome going to come about? What would your employees have to experience in order for you to create that organizational Experience? Perhaps you decide that they need to feel respected, listened to, valued, supported, and empowered to solve problems and act on opportunities. Now you are getting somewhere!

Once you have identified the Experience you intend to create, you know what direction your life needs to move in. The next big question is *What Mindset supports that Experience?* We will look at that in the next section of this book.

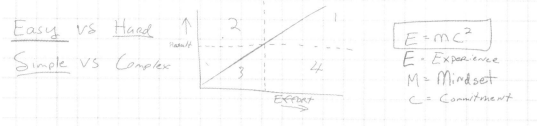

Easy vs Hard

Simple vs Complex

Result ↑

2

1

3

4

Effort →

$E = mc^2$

E = Experience

M = Mindset

C = Commitment

Part Three

Stepping into the Mindset

Commitment & Consistency

As a Leader, what "E" are you trying to maximize?

This is simple
It takes hard work
Commitment

Productivity ≠ Accountability

Accountability ⇒ Productivity

Chapter Thirteen

The "m" in
$E=mc^2$

"We cannot solve our problems with the same thinking we used in creating them."
—Albert Einstein

I WORK WITH A LOT OF BUSINESS LEADERS.
When I share the Theory of Accountability with them and describe the first element in the equation that supports it, Experience, I often hear this kind of response:

I'll tell you what kind of Experience I want to step into, Sam. I want to step into the Experience of leading the No. 1 company in this industry.

To which I always respond:

Great! Now you know the future you are creating. What MINDSET supports that future?

The second element of the Theory of Accountability formula—which is called Mindset—determines whether the Experience that we have visualized and set in motion with a present-tense *decision* will actually come into existence.

MINDSET BRINGS THE EXPERIENCE TO LIFE

Our chosen Mindset and our commitment to maintaining it and taking action on it are what bring the Experience to life.

In the second part of this book, we will look closely at the Mindset part of the equation...but I should point out before we get started that Mindset is intimately connected to Commitment. If we make a decision that points in one direction and sustain it with a Mindset to which we are not strongly Committed, we are not going to move in the direction of the future we aim to create. In fact, we may end up going in the opposite direction!

There is a lot to say about the power of Commitment, but before we spend too much time on that part of the equation, we need to look at which Mindset we are choosing and reinforcing to navigate the moment in front of us.

Your Mindset is what you believe at any given moment.

> **Your Mindset is what you believe at any given moment.**

Action always follows belief. Action determines what, if anything, you will achieve in support of your unique purpose. Belief is the engine that drives the action in your life and makes the compelling future you are envisioning possible. So it is extremely important to take time to critically examine what you believe about yourself, what you believe about other people, what you believe about the opportunities you face…and how those beliefs are actually showing up in terms of the choices you make and the actions you take.

What you believe about your world drives the action you take to create that world.

> What you believe about your world drives the action you take to create that world.

ARE WE WALKING OUR TALK?

Each of us has the task of determining for ourselves whether the beliefs we say we are following are actually expressing themselves in our words and deeds. Very often, we say that we believe one thing, but when we step back and take a look at what we are doing, we find that the words we say and the deeds we perform do not support our stated belief. In this situation, there is a mismatch, one that we need to notice and resolve. That resolution always begins with a close examination of our Mindset. *We do not believe what our actions undermine. If our actions do not support a stated belief, we do not really hold that belief.* And we need to notice that.

> If our actions do not support a stated belief, we do not hold that belief. And we need to notice that.

Let me give you a classic example of what I am talking about. Most company leaders I work with say that they believe in their people and trust them to make good decisions. Not all of them, however, actually believe this. How do I know that? Because their actions do not support their stated beliefs.

A while back, I was working with a CEO who led an organization that claimed to have as one of its core values the proposition that people were the company's greatest resource. At one point in our conversation, this executive looked me in the eye and said, "Sam, I have thirty-two problems, and every single one of them has a name." He was referring to his direct reports.

He could not possibly have been clearer about what his beliefs were—what his Mindset was. He believed that his people were a problem. End of story. That was his Mindset. As long as he held that belief, great things would be impossible for him, his team, and his organization.

He was trapped in three Toxic Mindsets I call Entitlement, Contempt, and Scarcity. Notice that another executive, with a different Mindset, one rooted in the belief that his people were capable of great things when supported properly, would be positioned to achieve truly extraordinary positive results *with the same thirty-two people.*

That is a proposition on which I would stake my career.

Chapter Fourteen

Three
Accountable Mindsets,
Three
Toxic Mindsets

"Service to others is the rent you pay
for your room here on earth."
—Muhammad Ali

THERE ARE THREE CRITICAL Accountable Mindsets that we can cultivate and use to strengthen our lives and our relationships with others. Let's look at each of them now—and also at each of their opposites. The opposites, the Toxic Mindsets, tend to show up by default when people do not make the conscious choice to design and employ an Accountable Mindset.

An Accountable Mindset yields a positive outcome, while a Toxic Mindset yields a negative outcome. This law is as reliable as any of the laws of physics.

THE FIRST ACCOUNTABLE MINDSET: GRATITUDE

Do you believe you are blessed?

Have you ever made a point of noticing when you have been on the receiving end of advantages and resources that others on the planet might not have easy access to—such as having enough food for yourself and your family? What about the ability to take a warm shower whenever you want, or to stay warm and dry in a snowstorm, or to go to sleep in a comfortable bed, or to make a room bright, even at nighttime, just by flicking a switch? In other words, have you ever noticed the good things that come your way in life? Do you feel and express authentic gratitude when someone helps you? Have you ever felt gratitude for things that you might have previously taken for granted, such as close relationships with friends, family members, and colleagues?

If you have ever experienced any of that, and I am guessing you have, then you were strengthening the Accountable Mindset known as *Gratitude*. Gratitude is an essential part of any healthy relationship, and it is an implied commitment to the people in our lives.

We hear the word *gratitude* often, but it is easy to lose sight of what it looks like in action. People who adopt the Mindset of Gratitude make other people feel special. They do this naturally and authentically, without having to think about *how* to make someone feel special, because they are grateful for a given person's presence in their life and their contributions, and they express that gratitude authentically. They have a way of making the conversation all about the other person—not all about them. They start from a commitment that sounds like this: "I would not be able to do what I do without you doing what you do—when you succeed, I succeed." And they are genuinely grateful for the contributions of others. (By the way, this is the commitment known as

"It's all of us" in action.) This appreciation is not contrived, not fake—it is an integral part of who they are and what they believe. They make you feel that they know you have made a positive difference in their life, and because of that, you feel good about interacting with them. You look forward to the next conversation and the next opportunity to contribute. Their gratitude makes *you* grateful to be in that person's orbit.

People who live in this Mindset know that everyone and everything is connected.

> **People who live in the Gratitude Mindset know that everyone and everything is connected.**

The opposite of *Gratitude* is the working assumption that you have an automatic right to resources, comforts, privileges, and relationships *without* experiencing any emotion of thankfulness for them. This is the Mindset of *Entitlement*, the polar opposite of Gratitude. A hallmark of *Entitlement,* which is a Toxic Mindset, is the belief that the world revolves around us and our desires, and that when something positive comes our way, we already had that gift coming, either as a result of our past actions or as a result of who we are.

People in the Entitlement Mindset tend to keep score about who got what, and they hold grudges when they do not receive something they think they deserve. Entitlement carries with it the assumption that agreements and commitments are something for other people to worry about, not something they have any obligation to take into account. As far as the entitled person is concerned, rules do not apply to them.

Accountable people choose a Mindset of Gratitude over a Mindset of Entitlement!

THE SECOND ACCOUNTABLE MINDSET: ABUNDANCE

Do you start from the assumption that there is enough for everybody? That a rising tide lifts all boats? That giving makes more of a positive impact on the world than taking? That when you look for, and find, something you can give to a person, a team, or an organization, everybody benefits? That the best way to support a relationship is to find something you can give to the other person in that relationship?

This is the Accountable Mindset of Abundance. It is the expression of the much-discussed principle that you get what you focus on giving. Many people refer to this idea as the Law of Attraction. I prefer to think of it as a basic principle of human fulfillment. I believe Abundance is our "factory setting"—we just lose sight of that sometimes. But we can always hit the reset button.

> There is something special that happens when you give, and give freely.

There is something special that happens when you give, and give freely. If you operate from the position that you are looking for opportunities to give without remorse, without feeling coerced—if you truly give from your heart—something opens up inside of you and new possibilities present themselves in support of the generosity you have initiated.

As you might expect, this Mindset shows up in the act of *giving*. People who live in an Abundance Mindset make a point of sharing freely of their time, their talents, and their treasures—meaning all their available resources.

> **People who live in an Abundance Mindset make a point of sharing freely of their time, their talents, and their treasures—meaning all their available resources.**

It is worth mentioning here that giving from a Mindset of Abundance does not mean making a decision to give because you already have a lot and you are willing to share what you think you will not be needing. It is making a decision to give because you know much has been given to you, because you believe the source of those gifts is limitless, and because you believe that what you have been given was given to you conditionally, not simply as a result of your efforts or merit. It was given to you on loan, with the understanding that you would take good care of the resources and pass them on to someone else. Another word for this Mindset is *Stewardship*. If you believe in Abundance, you believe that we come to this world empty-handed, we leave it empty-handed, and in the period in between those two events it is our job to be a good steward of the resources with which we have been entrusted. You do not worry about running out. If someone needs something and you feel you can make both of your lives better by giving it, you give it.

Not long ago, I came across the inspiring story of Leslie Lai, a restaurant owner in Hawaii whose business had been hit hard by the drop in foot traffic that followed the global pandemic. Lai was considering closing her doors, but she opted to operate the business at a loss for a time to maintain ties to her community. She also started making donations to a local food bank so as to support local people who were hit even harder than she had been. "We were so slow, but everyone was having problems with unemployment so I made the decision to keep the place open," she said. "Just trying to keep the family together." She described the choice to donate food from her restaurant to local charities, even when her own bottom line was in trouble, in similar terms: "We wanted to do something positive."[4] That is the Mindset of Abundance in action: *Doing something positive for others because you believe that is the right thing to do…not because it is convenient.*

The opposite of this Abundance Mindset is the operating assumption that there is not enough for everyone and that we are justified in grabbing what little is available for our own benefit. This is the Toxic Mindset of Scarcity. Scarcity is rooted in fear. It produces lack, desperation, and conflict. The Scarcity Mindset, and the unreasoning fear that drives it, can undermine and eventually destroy, not just working relationships, but all relationships. Fortunately, our fear can always be put in proper perspective by our purpose. As Malala, the brave Pakistani reformer for girls' education opportunities, so concisely put it:

"I am stronger than fear."
—Malala

This is the point from which she created new possibilities for millions of girls and for the educators who serve them. Toxic Mindsets

4.   Casey Lund, "Lava Nearly Claimed Her Home and COVID Left Her Unemployed Again, But She's Not Giving Up," *Hawaii News Now,* Gray Media Group, Inc., last updated March 25, 2021, https://www.hawaiinewsnow.com/2021/03/25/lava-nearly-claimed-her-home-covid-left-her-unemployed-again-shes-not-giving-up/.

run counter to the goal of helping people to reach their full potential by elevating them. When I am in a Scarcity Mindset, I am hoarding resources for myself rather than looking for ways to give them to you. When I am in an Abundance Mindset, I am creating new resources for everyone.

Accountable people choose a Mindset of Abundance over a Mindset of Scarcity!

THE THIRD ACCOUNTABLE MINDSET: RESPECT

Do you believe that other people have rights, just like you do? That their experiences and insights are as valid as your own? That all human beings have an inherent dignity and worth, regardless of any differences in culture, outlook, or belief system that may exist between them? Do you believe that people have a right to be treated well and that you should treat them as you yourself would want to be treated? Accountable leaders do. They are committed to a safe place to work—and that means, among other things, a workplace where respect is the norm.

They live in the Accountable Mindset of Respect. To live there, all you have to do is recognize that you are a human being, that one of the core requirements of human beings is connection with other human beings via functioning relationships, and that relationships function best for both parties when there is some aspect of respect on both sides. Ideally, this respect grows and develops over time. What does respect look like in action? What does it really mean? It means making sure that everyone has a seat at the table and that everyone at the table has a voice and a chance to speak, regardless of their rank, their department, their appearance, their level of influence within the group, or their age. Respect means accepting that every viewpoint matters, even if it is not one we happen to share. We may not always agree with what someone has to say, and we may not always be able to make everyone happy with our decisions, but we still need to ensure that the people with whom we come in contact are always encouraged to speak and are always heard with an open mind. That is what makes people feel respected.

> **People who live in a Respect Mindset accept that every viewpoint matters, even if it is not one they happen to share.**

Respect means looking the other person in the eye, regardless of whether they are wearing a three-piece suit or they are out on the street pushing around a shopping cart. It means interacting with people with authentic curiosity and compassion, whether or not they look like we do, talk like we do, or agree with us. It means accepting that no matter where people show up in the pecking order, they are a fellow human being, making the same cradle-to-grave journey we are making.

When we respect someone, we make an effort to learn what kinds of challenges that person is dealing with, even if they have dramatic differences with us in terms of perspective, background, or appearance. When we respect someone, we choose to work on the assumption that we are both members of the same human family and that we each deserve to be treated as such.

The opposite of this Mindset is the Toxic Mindset of Contempt. In this Mindset, we assume that the other person has no rights we are bound to observe, few or no feelings or insights we can benefit from understanding, and no aspirations we are obliged to understand.

When we consider another human being solely as a means to an end—our end—and we treat them accordingly, we are locked into the Toxic Mindset of Contempt.

When we consider another human being solely as a means to an end—our end—and we treat them accordingly, we are locked into the Toxic Mindset of Contempt.

Contempt is rooted in passing judgment on other people. This happens far more often than we think. Suppose we are waiting in line to purchase something, and the line is moving slower than we want it to, and we lean over and whisper to the person we are waiting in line with, "Just our luck—we had to come here on the day the high school dropout showed up for job training." Even if the person did not hear us, even if we think it is a joke, even if we tell ourselves we meant no harm, *we are passing judgment.* And that is contempt. And by the way—here is an important side note: the person you just leaned over and said that to could *be* a high school dropout, or could be the parent of a high school dropout, or could have a friend who is a high school dropout, or could simply have enough depth of character to realize that people who drop out of high school—like, say, John Lennon and Malcolm X—can make great contributions to the human family. In all of those situations, you just created a potentially painful gap in the conversation.

For the record, I know several people who left high school and started highly successful businesses. Just because something is not being done our way does not mean it is being done the wrong way! So we have to be careful about what we say. *Our words matter.* When they come from a place of contempt, when they unintentionally or purposefully hurt other people, they drag everyone down, including us!

Whenever someone starts a conversation out with a descriptor—a tag—about what another person looks like, where they come from, where they were educated, what their job is, what their intelligence level may or may not be, what their income level may or may not be, that is a precursor to judging that person. We may not think we are passing judgment on a person when we describe them in limiting terms, but we are. Not only that—if you are making a judgment on somebody based on a superficial factor like income, then you are also passing judgment on *everyone* who falls into that category. Think about that for a moment! Think about how much lost potential, how much division, how much needless acrimony, misunderstanding, and dysfunction follow us when we make a snap decision based on something external. Think about how much we lose out on when we use artificial categories to describe or dismiss people without bothering to determine who the human being we are dealing with really is. It is easier to do this than we realize. People do it all the time. Here is an example of a judgment that I hear on a regular basis: "So and so is making X dollars a year—that's a lot of money. They should know better than to make a mistake like that."

Think about what the person is really saying there: They are saying that wealthy people do not or should not make mistakes! And that people who do not make a lot of money are not as smart as, and make more mistakes than, people who do make a lot of money!

If that is the way we think, then there is contempt and bias in our life. That is a problem—a big one—that we need to address. Here is another all-too-common example of judgment and bias, both of which are rooted in contempt: a friend of mine recently heard a client say to him, "Your girl can take care of the proofreading on this project." Point number one: This client *knew* that the "girl" in question was a grown-up, not a child. Point number two: This client also knew that the "girl" was my friend's business partner—because my friend had mentioned that several times! That is contempt. In a situation like this, the other person may not realize it, but they are passing judgment on *all women* with a thoughtless, callous, insulting remark like that. Saying something like that does not just demean women—it demeans the speaker, and it demeans the person who lets the remark pass without comment. (My friend responded with, "Actually, she's not a girl; she's my partner.")

Very often, we do not recognize when we pass judgment on others. It is up to us to recognize when we are doing it in our own world and to make appropriate corrections when we notice it happening. If, during a meeting, someone asks us what Bob thinks of a certain idea, and we say, "Oh, Bob's just the receptionist," then *we have passed judgment on Bob,* and we need to figure out some way to address what we have done and make an appropriate adjustment, an adjustment that replaces contempt with respect. That may take the form of correcting ourselves instantly and saying, right out loud, "That word *just* I used a second ago was out of line, and it was unfair to Bob. He's not *just* the receptionist. He's not *just* anything. He's a member of the team, and I should not have dismissed his insights or his perspective." *Once respect is allowed to devolve into contempt because we have judged someone unfairly, then we need to acknowledge what has happened, own it, and find a way to fix it and make sure the behavior does not show up again.*

As soon as we pass judgment on another person, our respect for that person vanishes and contempt takes over.

> As soon as we pass judgment on another person, our respect for that person vanishes and contempt takes over.

Every time we pass judgment, we are setting up a comparison between "us" and "them"—coming up with arguments that support the idea that we are better and they are worse, or that we are more qualified and they are less qualified, or that we are more intelligent and they are less intelligent, or that our opinion is closer to right and theirs is closer to wrong. That is contempt.

Very often, habits of passing judgment and exhibiting contempt show up in our lives because *that is how we were taught to socialize:* to pass judgment on one person or groups of people in order to score social points with another person or groups of people. If that is the case, we need to acknowledge that passing judgment is what happened and we need to learn new ways to socialize that do not come at someone else's expense—because every time we pass judgment, that sets the stage for contempt; and every time we show contempt, we steep ourselves in a dysfunctional Mindset, a Mindset that makes respect impossible. Every time we step into the Toxic Mindset of Contempt, we not only devalue others, we devalue ourselves.

Accountable people choose a Mindset of Respect over a Mindset of Contempt!

MINDSET IS A MATTER OF CHOICE!

Whether we realize it or not, our Mindset is a matter of choice. If we choose to step into a Respect Mindset, we will not have a Contempt Mindset. If we choose to step into an Abundance Mindset, we will not have a Scarcity Mindset. If we choose to step into a Gratitude Mindset, we will not have an Entitlement Mindset.

> If we choose to step into a Respect Mindset, we will not have a Contempt Mindset. If we choose to step into an Abundance Mindset, we will not have a Scarcity Mindset. If we choose to step into a Gratitude Mindset, we will not have an Entitlement Mindset.

The minute we make the choice to allow our Mindset to slip from Accountable to Toxic, everything around us changes for the worse. The minute we make the choice to move our mindset from Toxic back to Accountable, everything around us changes for the better.

An important word of guidance is in order here: the *only* Mindset you can choose is your own. You are in charge of *your* Mindset. You are not in charge of, nor can you control, anyone else's Mindset.

If someone in your circle is (or seems to be) clinging to a Toxic Mindset and is communicating accordingly, here are some questions to ask yourself before you try to administer an ill-advised "attitude adjustment":

- Are you sure you know the whole story? (It is possible there is something going on in this person's life that makes it hard for them to move into an Accountable Mindset. When unsure, why not give the person the benefit of the doubt and content yourself with setting a good example? You do not know what they are up against.)

- Are you sure you will make the situation better, rather than worse, if you engage with the other person about the importance of changing their Mindset of Contempt, Scarcity, and/or Entitlement? (Usually, telling other people that they need to change their Mindset backfires. If the person has not asked you for help in learning to adopt an Accountable Mindset, why offer it?)

- Is there really an issue here? (There may not be. Very often, people convince themselves that they are trying to "improve" others...but they are really putting their own ego in the driver's seat. Why run the risk of being that person? If you can move on without any adverse impact to anyone, move on. If this is really about improving your image or settling scores, move on.)

Yes, you can speak your truth. Yes, you can set boundaries. Yes, you can be frank about what you do and do not condone in your space. But you can do all of that without buying into a Toxic Mindset and accelerating (or creating) a cycle of pointless conflict.

Chapter Fifteen

Accountable Mindsets Take Practice; Toxic Mindsets Are Easy

"The path of least resistance leads to crooked rivers and crooked men."
—Henry David Thoreau

UNFORTUNATELY, we *all* can find ourselves making choices that leave us operating from one or more of the Toxic Mindsets. Making toxicity our default setting is all too easy, especially if the people around us have a habit of using one or more of the three Toxic Mindsets.

> Making toxicity our default setting is all too easy, especially if the people around us have a habit of using one or more of the three Toxic Mindsets. Choose to surround yourself with people who embrace the Accountable Mindsets.

Social influences can convince us that acting entitled, envisioning scarcity, and/or showing contempt is justifiable, or even expected, behavior. If you spend even a few minutes online monitoring any social media feed, I predict you will quickly encounter all three Toxic Mindsets. Let's face it: they are pervasive in our society, which means it is extremely easy for people to bond over them and even make them expected parts of their important relationships.

I want to challenge you now to take a closer look at this cycle. Back when we were in school, some kids would pick on other kids for the fun of it…and also because they believed insulting and attacking others made them the center of attention and gave them higher social status. They liked that attention and that status. As adults, we can recognize that that is an unhealthy pattern of behavior, something that kids need to be coached through so that they can make better choices. But here's the thing: For some people, this pattern did not stop in school. It kept going right into adulthood, and the fact that the cycle now plays out in front of the water cooler, or online, does not change the toxicity and the unhealthiness of the cycle. It is still Contempt. And we need to learn to disengage from it.

The three Accountable Mindsets we just examined usually take practice and support from a carefully chosen group of people in order for us to make them our standard operating procedure. There are far fewer steady practitioners of the Accountable Mindsets than there are Toxic Mindset specialists. If we want to make accountability a consistent pattern in our life and in our decision-making, we will need to start by making different choices about who and what we surround ourselves with.

I avoid people who indulge in the three Toxic Mindsets and consider indulging in those Mindsets "normal," and I urge you to avoid them as well.

> Toxic Mindsets are not healthy, no matter how easy it may be for us to slip into using them. Accountable Mindsets always lead us in the right direction.

These ways of looking at the world are not healthy. Long years of habit may have persuaded us that they are acceptable, but they are not, no matter how used to them we may be or how easily they may slip into our interactions with, or our assessments of, others. Look once again at what the CEO I mentioned had to say about his team, and notice that he was trapped in not one, not two, but all three of the Toxic Mindsets I have shared with you.

"Sam, I have thirty-two problems, and every single one of them has a name."

Does this remark show GRATITUDE for the talents and experiences of the people who have chosen to work for this man? No, quite the contrary. This is ENTITLEMENT, the belief that the world revolves around us and what we want, the belief that we are justified in keeping score and holding grudges. Entitlement often expresses itself at the top of the organization in sentiments like this:

I'm paying that person to do the job—they should do it without expecting a pat on the back. I show my appreciation by making sure a paycheck shows up each Friday.

If you want a friend, get a dog.

If you can't stand the heat, get out of the kitchen.

Moving on: Does the CEO's complaint about the thirty-two problems come from a place of ABUNDANCE? Does it focus on what has been accomplished and what could be accomplished? Does it focus on opportunity? Does it open doors? No, it is all about SCARCITY: each direct report not only *causes* problems, but *is* a problem! That is not who I want to work for, and I doubt that it is who you want to work for, either. In the mind of an executive like this, he or she is the only one who can come up with solutions—not the thirty-two people. This (so-called) leader sees scarcity everywhere: scarcity in creativity, scarcity in talent, and scarcity in potential when it comes to dealing with the kinds of problems that are going to come up in any organization. And that scarcity is what shows up. Why? Because you always find what you look for.

Does this remark show evidence of RESPECT for the direct reports as human beings? Absolutely not. The employees are seen by the supposed leader as means to an end, not as human beings with their own needs, aspirations, and capabilities. There is potential waiting to be discovered in each of those thirty-two direct reports, but this executive will not find it because he is far more comfortable with Contempt. People who say these kinds of things about others often hide behind the fact that they do not say the toxic things they think right to the other person's face. They ignore the reality that what they have said is disrespectful *whether the person hears it or not*. Contempt is, by definition, disrespectful whether it is spoken to the person in question or to someone else.

> Toxic Mindsets are easy—and destructive. Accountable Mindsets take practice—and they strengthen relationships.

Chapter Sixteen

What We Need to Notice about Mindset

"Our life is shaped by our mind, for we become what we think." —Buddha

IT IS ALWAYS up to us to notice whether the Mindset we have chosen to step into is Accountable or Toxic, just like it is always up to us which direction a car is heading when we are driving it.

> It is always up to us to notice whether the Mindset we have chosen to step into is Accountable or Toxic, just like it is always up to us which direction a car is heading when we are driving it.

Our life is always heading in one of two directions: toward being ON PURPOSE or toward being OFF PURPOSE. It is like driving a car on a highway. A highway runs in two directions; you get to choose which direction you are going. The vehicle on the highway can be heading only in one direction, not two, at any given instant. *We choose the direction of our journey in every waking moment.* And we want to make sure we are heading in the direction we really want to go.

When we make a conscious effort to cultivate one of the three Accountable Mindsets, we are moving toward being ON PURPOSE. Why? Because our Mindset—our beliefs—determine our actions, and our actions are much, much more likely to align with our purpose when we choose to take on a Mindset of Abundance, Gratitude, and Respect. By the same token, a great way to go OFF PURPOSE is to cultivate a Mindset of Scarcity, Entitlement, or Contempt. Driving the car in that direction inevitably leads to actions that *do not* align with our purpose.

All of us sometimes operate from an Accountable Mindset, and *all of us* sometimes operate from a Toxic Mindset. The trick is not simply to "think positively" but to *be aware* of what we are thinking.

> The trick is not simply to "think positively" but to be aware of what we are thinking.

It is our job to *notice* when we are slipping into beliefs and actions that reflect Scarcity and then make a conscious choice to replace those with beliefs and actions that reflect Abundance.

It is our job to *notice* when we are slipping into beliefs and actions that reflect Entitlement and then make a conscious choice to replace those with beliefs and actions that reflect Gratitude.

It is our job to *notice* when we are slipping into beliefs and actions that reflect Contempt and then make a conscious choice to replace those with beliefs and actions that reflect Respect.

SIX IMPORTANT THINGS ACCOUNTABLE PEOPLE KNOW ABOUT MINDSET

There are six important things accountable people know about Mindset:

- **ONE: Your Mindset is what you believe** about yourself, the world, and other people.

- **TWO: Your Mindset is always with you.** Even if you think your Mindset does not affect your perceptions and decisions, it does.

- **THREE: At any given moment, your Mindset is either Toxic or Accountable.** There is no middle ground. It is always one or the other, and where you land on that is up to you.

- **FOUR: There are three, and only three, Accountable Mindsets.** The flip side of each Accountable Mindset is a Toxic Mindset. This means there are three Mindset Transitions that accountable people learn to make:

TOXIC	→	ACCOUNTABLE
SCARCITY	→	ABUNDANCE
ENTITLEMENT	→	GRATITUDE
CONTEMPT	→	RESPECT

- **FIVE: Choosing to live in an Accountable Mindset supports and deepens your commitment to your relationships.** Choosing to live in a Toxic Mindset degrades your commitment to your relationships.

- **SIX: Your Mindset is always a matter of choice.** You always have the choice of making it Toxic or making it Accountable. Many people make this choice unconsciously or semi-consciously and lean toward the Toxic. Accountable people, on the other hand, make the choice consciously, because they are committed to developing themselves and other people to the highest and best level of potential possible…and they know that a Toxic Mindset is incompatible with that commitment.

There are three, and only three, Accountable Mindsets. The flip side of each Accountable Mindset is a Toxic Mindset. This means there are three Mindset Transitions that accountable people learn to make:

TOXIC	→	ACCOUNTABLE
SCARCITY	→	ABUNDANCE
ENTITLEMENT	→	GRATITUDE
CONTEMPT	→	RESPECT

Notice that the three *Toxic* Mindsets are all about *me*...and the three *Accountable* Mindsets are all about *us*. This is because accountability is focused on supporting relationships by means of *service*. Notice, too, that when you take on an Accountable Mindset, you apply it to yourself as well as to the people you serve. You, too, deserve Abundance. You, too, deserve Gratitude. You, too, deserve Respect. Many people are too hard on themselves. Don't be one of those people!

Ultimately, accountability is about relationships. Very often, when people think about accountability, they think about *tactical* commitments, about a specific, narrowly defined task—for instance, taking out the trash. They think, *I said I was going to take out the trash, then I did, so therefore I am accountable.* Nope. That's responsibility, not accountability. It is not the actions themselves that make you accountable. It is you making your word your bond that makes you accountable!

The point is, maintaining an Accountable Mindset means focusing your attention on keeping *relational* commitments. These are not to-do items you cross off a list and then pat yourself on the back for completing. These are *long-term, ongoing commitments to the quality of your relationship with at least one other person.*

This is a question of intention, and yes, acting with the right intention takes practice. Just as a marathon runner does not start out by running twenty-six miles the first time, people who are really, really good at sustaining an Accountable Mindset do not start out by expecting to maintain that Mindset all, or even most, of the time. This is the work of a lifetime. By simply noticing Scarcity, Entitlement, and Contempt when they show up, and replacing them with their Accountable counterparts—Abundance, Gratitude, and Respect—without beating ourselves up, we build up the Accountability Mindset muscle. And that is a good thing to do, because *nobody can build up that muscle but us.*

> By simply noticing Scarcity, Entitlement, and Contempt when they show up, and replacing them with their Accountable counterparts—Abundance, Gratitude, and Respect—without beating ourselves up, we build up the Accountability Mindset muscle.

Where we are likely to need help along the way is not with the building up of the muscle but with the noticing. I call the moments where we notice what kind of Mindset we are in, and then start thinking about what kind of Mindset we want to occupy, *Choice Points*. We always have a choice. It is recognizing those Choice Points when they show up that empowers us.

This is where mentors and accountability partners come in. They can help us to get better at noticing the Choice Points. It is only human to look for, and find, ways to convince ourselves that a Scarcity Mindset is really something constructive, something we call *being realistic*. By the same token, we may persuade ourselves that an Entitlement Mindset is really something helpful, something we call *getting what I deserve*. And we may even convince ourselves that a Contempt Mindset is really something designed to help others, something we call *giving them a reality check*.

Very often, *we do not understand what Mindset we have really taken on*. And that is one of the major things we need mentors for: to help us gain clarity about whether we are really in an Accountable Mindset or a Toxic Mindset, because it is surprisingly easy to get them mixed up.

For instance: Many entrepreneurs and business leaders find themselves falling into a combination of the Contempt and Scarcity Mindsets that expresses itself in thoughts like this:

If I want it done right, I have to do it myself!

With the help of a mentor and/or an accountability partner, entrepreneurs and other business leaders can learn to spot this common toxic thought pattern for what it is—a trap that will keep them from growing their business and growing as an individual. Here is the Accountable alternative, which is rooted in Respect and Abundance Mindsets:

The people around me bring unique skill sets and abilities to the table. They each have different growth trajectories, but as a group I know they can solve problems and help me achieve what I am trying to achieve...if I empower them. I can empower them by letting them know that I believe in them and by offering them opportunities for growth. Once I do that, I'll be unleashing a powerful competitive weapon.

Noticing the toxicity of the first thought pattern, taking advantage of the Choice Point, and turning the toxic mantra into an accountable alternative is what the Mindset part of the Accountability Equation is all about.

If you are like me and you want to get better at this, you will want to start by acknowledging the possibility that the choice to slip into a Toxic Mindset may have built up momentum in your life as a result of habit, inattention, and social pressure. If that is where you are, take comfort in the knowledge that that is where most of us are...and read the next chapter carefully.

Chapter Seventeen

Four Simple Things You Can Do to Ensure Your Mindset Is Accountable

"The mind is just like a muscle. The more you exercise it, the stronger it gets, and the more it can expand." —Idowu Koyenikan

HERE ARE FOUR SIMPLE, PAINLESS STEPS you can take over the next twenty-four hours to make it easier to live more of your life in an Accountable Mindset. Do not move on to the next chapter until you have taken them!

- **Find a mentor and/or an accountability partner.** Share this book with that person. Check in with him or her once a week or more. Start a discussion about the Experience you are creating and the Mindset that supports it.

- **Start your day by finding ways to reinforce Gratitude, Respect, and Abundance in your life.** Build in five to ten minutes of purposeful reflection about what, specifically, you are grateful for, whom you respect, and what kind of abundance—financial, physical, spiritual, and emotional—you are committed to bringing into the lives of others today. Some people do this by means of writing in a journal. Some people do it through meditation. Some people do it during conversations with a spouse or loved one. Whatever works for you, do it. Use this time at the beginning of your day to ask, *How do I bring Gratitude, Respect, and Abundance into my life today?*

- **Set aside some time during your day when your "digital feed" is off.** Cell phones, computers, televisions, and other portals into electronic stimulation may leave you open to professional manipulators who reap financial rewards by sending messages that instill mindsets of Scarcity, Contempt, and Entitlement. Give these media sources a break for at least part of your day. I recommend setting aside some time when you have no exposure to outside media. You can use this time to communicate all you want with people in person or via real-time videoconference or phone calls. Just skip the parts where you are watching videos, reading posts, or reacting to the latest carefully designed opportunity for you to express contempt, feel entitled, or fear scarcity at the same time as millions of other people.

- **Limit or eliminate the amount of time you spend with people who have addicted themselves to Toxic Mindsets.** People who have proven to you through their actions that they do not want to break themselves of that addiction should not be getting large chunks of your day.

Our beliefs shape the results in our lives. If we want different results, we must change what we believe about a given person, a given situation, or a given opportunity from Toxic to Accountable. That means changing our Mindset and thereby changing our actions.

We are responsible for every single outcome in our lives—no exceptions. If we want different outcomes, we have to change what we BELIEVE about a given person, a given situation, or a given opportunity from Toxic to Accountable. That means changing our Mindset and thereby changing our actions.

Chapter Eighteen

What Do You Really Believe?

"When you are able to maintain your own highest standards of integrity, regardless of what others may do, you are destined for greatness." —Napoleon Hill

A LOT OF TIMES we may think we have one Mindset, but we really are living in another. Our words may say we believe one thing, but our actions may not always support those beliefs. When this happens, we need to clarify what we believe.

When I am facing a big decision, and for whatever reason I am about to embark on a course of action that does not match up well with my stated purpose, a good friend of mine will ask me, as many times as necessary: "Is that what you really believe?" At first, I found this habit irritating. Now I see it for what it is: an opportunity to align my beliefs, my Mindset, with my actions and my purpose. Very often, what I find is that a course of action I am considering taking is rooted in a Toxic

Mindset (Scarcity, let's say) and that a whole different opportunity—in fact, a whole different way of living—is waiting for me once I take on the opposite Mindset (Abundance).

To illustrate what I mean, let me go back to our example of that young Navy veteran running for Congress in his very first political race, back in 1946: John F. Kennedy. At one point in that campaign, young Kennedy was to address a crowded room but was informed before he went on that the public address system was not functioning. Would he be willing to give the speech without a microphone?

At first, Kennedy's Mindset was one of Scarcity. He focused on what he believed he *did not* have: a working microphone, experience, the ability to command attention, a good speaking voice. He told the organizer of the event that he could not deliver the speech and got ready to leave the venue. At that point, the candidate's mentor—Joseph P. Kennedy, his father—had a talk with him. We do not know exactly what was said, but given what we know about the senior Kennedy's ability to reframe his son's perspective with regard to speaking ability, I am willing to bet that the conversation pointed the candidate toward what he *did* have, toward what was *possible*, *happening*, and *positive* in that room full of people waiting eagerly to hear the speech. In short, I believe the mentor reframed the mentee's beliefs about the situation. I believe he changed the candidate's Mindset from one of Scarcity to one of Abundance.

Kennedy gave the speech, which was well received. That night, he learned an important lesson about Mindset…and about possibility.

In the moment when he had convinced himself that what mattered was what he *did not* have, Kennedy was doubtless fixated on questions like these:

What if I make a fool of myself?

Why should I go out there and embarrass my family and myself?

What if people start to leave—or start to boo—when I start speaking?

But in the moment of possibility, the moment when his Mindset became one of Abundance, he would have been far more likely to fix his mind on questions like these:

What have I experienced in my life that will inspire others?

What can I contribute to the lives of the people in this room?

How can I make a positive impact on this group, on Massachusetts, on the country, and on the world?

The first set of questions are the product of a Scarcity Mindset. The second set of questions are the product of an Abundance Mindset. Fortunately, Kennedy had a mentor—his father—who helped him that night to push past beliefs that were rooted in Scarcity. His beliefs changed. His decisions changed. And his actions changed. So his outcome changed! The focus changed from Kennedy *himself* to *how he could serve other people.* This is the key. To adopt an Accountable Mindset, we need to make the transition from *self* to *service.*

> To adopt an Accountable Mindset, we need to make the transition from self to service.

I work with a lot of executives. Many of them are highly goal-oriented, and of course I have no problem with that. Having a mission means being willing to set and pursue compelling, powerful goals. I sometimes have to remind executives, though, that their goal-orientation is unsustainable if it does not connect to this concept of *service.*

If your aim is to use the Theory of Accountability to grow your business or advance your career, that is great. Just remember as you identify the Mindset that supports your goals that you are eventually going to want to connect your Mindset and your actions back to *people* at some point. There is absolutely no problem with setting an audacious financial or career goal, as long as you remember that that goal is the beginning, not the end, of the conversation. If you have decided that you want your team to generate ten million dollars in sales and you know that is the Experience you want to create, congratulations! That is a great benchmark to shoot for. But do not make the mistake of stopping there. Whom are the people on your sales team (and elsewhere in your organization) going to *serve* by attaining that sales goal? How will they serve those people? How will *you* serve the people who report to you as they take on that goal of service?

Whenever you take your Mindset out of *service* mode, you risk beginning the slide toward mediocrity—or worse. The worst situation I have ever faced professionally came when I agreed to deliver a program that I knew, deep down, was a bad fit for a client of mine. The program in question was not my idea but the client's. I persuaded myself that the program might not end up being a total disaster…but it was.

Why did I let the client talk me into delivering that program? Because I wanted the money. I wanted to close the deal because I thought I needed the cash.

Do you see what happened there? I stopped serving the client. If I had been serving the client, I would have pushed back and refused to deliver a program I knew would not work for them. Why did I stop serving the client? Because I had slipped into a Scarcity Mindset.

ARE YOU LOOKING TO GET, OR ARE YOU LOOKING TO GIVE?

When we move from a fearful Mindset of Scarcity to a generous Mindset of Abundance, the moment we are living in changes from being all about us to being all about those we can serve. It is like that with the other two Toxic Mindsets as well: they are focused on *self*. When we transition into accountability, we leave Contempt behind and move into Respect for others. When we transition into accountability, we leave Entitlement behind and move into showing authentic Gratitude for the good things in our lives, starting with people and relationships. I believe that *all* the positive Mindsets open to us connect to these three basic shifts in perspective. I believe that choosing an Accountable Mindset means choosing to give, rather than get. That takes practice. But mastering these three accountable ways of looking at the world is definitely worth the effort.

If Kennedy had stopped giving speeches in public right after that night in 1946 when he spoke without a microphone…if he had allowed a Scarcity Mindset, or some other Toxic Mindset, to creep in once again and direct his decisions…if he had put a halt to his personal growth as a speaker, a candidate, a leader, and a human being…what would that have cost the rest of us? Would we have gotten the famous inaugural address in 1961 when he challenged us to ask not what our country could do for us, but what we could do for our country? Would he have electrified a hundred thousand Berliners trapped behind the Berlin Wall by informing them that he was one of them? Would he have challenged a nation to send a man to the moon and return him to earth safely, thereby setting in motion one of humankind's greatest achievements?

Of course not. One good speech, one instance of overcoming a Toxic Mindset, one truly accountable action was not going to be enough for Kennedy to fulfill his own potential and his own purpose. He needed *hundreds* of speeches, *thousands* of speeches in order to become the person he was capable of becoming. Nothing worthy of our true potential as human beings comes about without sustained effort; without continuous, purposeful *action*. And this truth brings us face to face with the third element in the Accountability Equation, *Commitment*, which is what we will be looking at in the next section of the book.

Chapter Nineteen

Put What You Have Learned about the "m" in E=mc² into Practice!

"Love challenges, be intrigued by mistakes, enjoy effort, and keep on learning."
—Carol Dweck

NOW THAT YOU HAVE LEARNED about Mindset, you are ready to take the next step. Here are some powerful questions about Mindset for you to consider. The more detailed your answers, the better prepared you will be to put what you know into practice.

- Think of something that you were in charge of that did not go well. What beliefs about yourself, other people, and the world at large might have contributed to the disappointing outcome? (Example: As I mentioned in the previous chapter, I agreed to deliver a program that I knew was not a good fit for a client. Why? Because I had slipped into a Scarcity Mindset. I wanted the sale, and I stopped thinking about how best to serve my client. The program bombed.)

- What is a specific moment when you allowed yourself to slip into the Toxic Mindset of Contempt? (Be honest with yourself about this—we have all done it.)

- How would the Accountable Mindset of Respect have expressed itself in that situation?

- What is a specific moment when you allowed yourself to slip into the Toxic Mindset of Entitlement? (Again, be honest with yourself.)

- How would the Accountable Mindset of Gratitude have expressed itself in that situation?

- What is a specific moment when you allowed yourself to slip into the Toxic Mindset of Scarcity? (Tell the truth.)

- How would the Accountable Mindset of Abundance have expressed itself in that situation?

- Think of an Experience you chose to step into in Part Two of this book. Pick an Experience that is important to you personally. Which Accountable Mindset most supports that Experience? How will you take it on? When would you be tempted to slip into the Toxic counterpart of that Mindset? How will you respond when you find yourself in a situation that triggers that Toxic Mindset?

- When you are faced with an obstacle to that Experience that you cannot control, what can you do to assume full control of your Mindset? What specific steps will you take to embrace that Mindset? For instance: Does physical exercise make it easier for you to enter an Accountable Mindset? Does taking a deep breath? Does disengaging for a moment and giving yourself permission to think of all the people and resources in your life you are grateful for, the people you respect most, or the abundance you are privileged to share with others? (Note that you *always* have control over your Mindset, no matter what else may be out of your control.)

- Think of a time when someone in your world showed up with a Toxic Mindset (examples: Contempt, Scarcity, Entitlement). How did that make you feel? What did you do, or could you do, to keep your own Mindset Accountable? How could you have inspired that person to adopt an Accountable Mindset?

- Who is your personal role model when it comes to sustaining the Mindset of Abundance? What do they do that makes you think of them as role models? What can you do to be more like them when it comes to living in that Mindset?

- Who is your personal role model when it comes to sustaining the Mindset of Respect? What do they do that makes you think of them as role models? What can you do to be more like them when it comes to living in that Mindset?

- Who is your personal role model when it comes to sustaining the Mindset of Gratitude? What do they do that makes you think of them as role models? What can you do to be more like them when it comes to living in that Mindset?

The next few questions are meant for leaders and entrepreneurs. It is quite common for these people to identify an Experience like the following: "I want us to be a $50 million company by the thirty-first of December of this year." Although I generally prefer to start with the relationships, I want to be very clear, once again, that there is nothing wrong with choosing something like this as your Experience, as long as you recognize three critical things:

1. *Your Mindset is ultimately going to determine whether you are able to step into that future you have chosen,* because it is your Mindset that will determine the quality of your relationships, and relationships are essential to any organizational goal.

2. *While financial success is important, on its own money is not your purpose.* So you will still need to connect the dots and determine *why* you want a $50 million company and specifically whom you are serving by leading such a company, if you expect to sustain a Mindset that supports your goals. Yes, you need money to run your business. You also need to breathe in order to keep your body functioning. But breathing is not your purpose in life, and earning money is not your organization's purpose. Keep thinking about whom you serve and why you serve them. Make it about more than money. When you make it only about the money, you will make some money. But when you know your Why and you make it about more than the money, you will make *more* money.

3. *Accountability is always about keeping your commitments to people.* It is about supporting and deepening relationships, and it always starts with you, the leader.

Having established that much, you can start to look at the following important questions about Mindset and team performance (these questions are specifically designed for leaders who are accountable to teams in the workplace):

- What would you have to believe about yourself, the world you live in, and the people you serve (specifically, your employees) in order to attain this performance goal? For instance, you would have to believe that the goal of $50 million in income by December 31 is attainable (an Abundance Mindset), and you would also have to believe that the team you have in place is capable of achieving it...and of coming up with creative solutions to the challenges that will inevitably arise along the way (Abundance and Respect). And you would also have to believe that you can and should give things like training, fair compensation, commitment to their well-being, and ongoing emotional support to your people (Gratitude) if you expect them to be fully committed to the organizational goal that is important to you.

- Now flip that around and ask yourself: What beliefs would stand in the way of your organization reaching $50 million in revenues by the target date? Obviously, believing that the goal is impossible (Scarcity) is going to shut down the possibility of your organization being where you want it to be. By the same token, a default belief that your team members cannot possibly do the job and are incapable of solving basic problems on their own (Scarcity, Contempt) is going to shut you down just as fast. By the way, whose issue is it really if the wrong people have been hired, onboarded, under-trained, and assigned the wrong projects in support of that $50 million goal? Yours!

- What kind of company culture would you need to have to attain these goals? What values would support such a culture? Do you know what they are? Do you live those values? Do you evangelize them? Do you demonstrate exactly what those values look like in action in every decision and every interaction with your team members?

By now, you should have a clear grasp of the Experience and Mindset elements of the Accountability Equation. You are ready to take a deep dive into the final element, the one that makes your desired Experience a reality: Commitment.

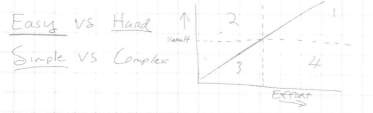

Easy vs Hard

Simple vs Complex

Result ↑

2

3

4

1

Effort →

$E = mc^2$

E = Experience

M = Mindset

C = Commitment

Part Four

Commitment—
Swinging
the Hammer

Commitment ≠ Consistency

As a Leader, what "E"
are you trying to maximize?

This is simple.
It takes hard work
Commitment

Productivity ≠ Accountability

Accountability ⟹ Productivity

Chapter Twenty

The "c" in $E=mc^2$: Commitment

"There's a difference between interest and commitment. When you're interested in doing something, you do it only when circumstances permit. When you're committed to something, you accept no excuses, only results." —Art Turock

THIS PART OF THE BOOK is all about *action*.

The third part of the Accountability Equation is Commitment. Commitment is taking action in a purposeful way, repeatedly and relentlessly. Along the way, check your compass to ensure that you are fulfilling your purpose. But act!

> **Commitment is taking action in a purposeful way, repeatedly and relentlessly.**

Choosing the Experience, the future you want to step into, is essential, but it is not enough. Choosing your Mindset, taking stock of what you believe and ensuring that it is Accountable, not Toxic, is also essential—but it is not enough. At some point, you do need an implementation plan, and you do need to execute it. Commitment is what makes that happen.

Think of it this way: putting the Theory of Accountability into action is a little bit like building a house. Commitment—the relentless action you are willing to take—is the hammer. The right Mindset—the Accountable Mindset—is the nail. And the Experience you are stepping into, the future you are creating, is the house you are building with every swing of the hammer.

When you are building a house and pounding in a nail, you have to pound it more than once. You have to keep the hammer swinging!

> **Commitment is the hammer. Keep the hammer swinging!**

THE COMMITMENT MATRIX

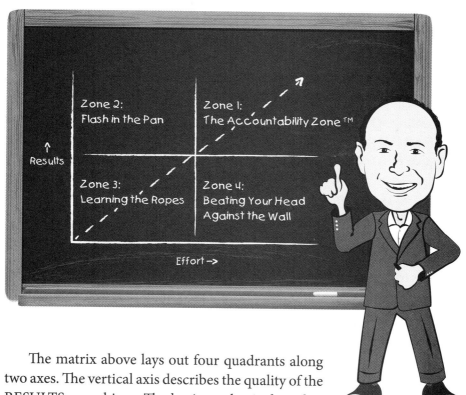

The matrix above lays out four quadrants along two axes. The vertical axis describes the quality of the RESULTS we achieve. The horizontal axis describes the amount of EFFORT we put in. (By "effort" I mean an action we can count and measure the outcome of, not simply busy work.) Notice the direction the performance line goes—it is diagonal! It does not shoot straight up. Some people expect a tiny amount of effort to deliver a quality result—but that is not how it works. We have to keep at it over time.

Truly successful people—on the playing field, in the workplace, and everywhere else—make it their aim to live in the upper right-hand corner of this quadrant: HIGH-QUALITY results (meaning execution that aligns with our purpose and improves as we learn more and do more), accompanied by CONSISTENT, RELENTLESS EFFORT. I call this quadrant the Accountability Zone™.

The Accountability Zone™ is where Jackie Robinson spent most of his time—at a consistently high level of execution and a relentless, unceasing level of activity. No matter the obstacle, he did not make or accept excuses. He simply never stopped analyzing, improving, and executing at a consistently high level. He did not listen to the skepticism or hostility of others. He did not bother himself about whether others belittled his goal of *creating an environment where African Americans could be seen as the equals of other Americans—where they could compete fairly, be judged on their abilities, and be rewarded for their accomplishments.* He did not trouble himself with whether other people thought that goal was unrealistic. He did not compromise on the standards he set for himself, and he did not compromise on the continuous level of effort necessary to execute at those high standards, over and over and over again.

Malala, the young reformer for educational equality, showed the same level of relentless Commitment to the Experience in her choices to organize and to speak out publicly in support of educational opportunities for girls, even at the risk of her own life. Just as Robinson did, she has received countless death threats for maintaining her level of Commitment. But she continues to operate in the Accountability Zone, taking relentless action in support of her chosen Experience—*a world where every girl can learn and lead.*

"I think of it often and imagine the scene clearly. Even if they come to kill me, I will tell them what they are trying to do is wrong, that education is our basic right." —Malala

Picture Jackie Robinson relentlessly focusing on and executing his game plan in 1947, stepping into the batter's box knowing that every base hit, every base runner advanced, every stolen base brought him closer to the fulfillment of his mission, and you will see the image of the Accountability Zone. Picture Malala taking the world stage, not once, but over and over again, to advocate for the rights of girls in all nations to receive an education, and you will see the image of the Accountability Zone. You will see someone ON PURPOSE, on a mission, and taking relentless action in support of that mission.

That is where we want to be—in the Accountability Zone, swinging away at the ball with consistent action and execution that improves over time, regardless of the challenges we face. That ball we are swinging at can be anything, as long as it:

- Connects to our purpose

- Does not violate the rights of others

- Engages us and inspires us to accelerate our actions in support of the Experience we have chosen and the Mindset we have embraced

Once we are swinging away at something that meets all three of these criteria, *we are harnessing the exponential power of Commitment.* This is what is happening in Zone 1. I call the steady, energizing increase of focused effort in this quadrant THE HAMMER. How often do you swing the hammer, and how hard, and to what end? That is up to you.

While it would be nice if we were always operating in the Accountability Zone, always swinging THE HAMMER, the reality is that we are human beings, and sometimes we will not hit that standard. We are going to have good days and bad days. The point is to *return* to the Accountability Zone, not to expect that we will never leave it. So, what is happening in the other three zones of the matrix?

Well, in Zone 2, we see the pattern of high-quality but sporadic or inconsistent effort. This is the person who hits the ball once or twice during a practice session, likes how far it goes, but then runs into an obstacle. That obstacle might be discrimination. It might be a lack of capital. It might be a desire to emulate or please people in our circle who spend time in the Toxic Mindsets of Contempt, Entitlement, and Scarcity.

There are countless potential obstacles waiting for us. Each one connects to an excuse about why we cannot move forward and to a complaint about why the world has not given us more than it has. This is the zone of inconsistent Commitment and unfulfilled potential. It is where we accept the lie that someone or something else is in charge of the outcomes we produce in our life. This zone does not take us anywhere we want to go. It is the easiest of the three zones to move into Zone 1 from, because all we need to do is ramp up the activity level—the effort. Yes, sometimes we land in Zone 2, but if we choose to stay in this zone rather than picking up THE HAMMER and moving up to the Accountability Zone where we belong, we are one of those people who are asking for "unfulfilled potential" to be written on our tombstone. This is why I call this zone FLASH IN THE PAN.

The lower left-hand corner is Zone 3. Here is where we see low-quality execution and inconsistent effort. This is either the zone of getting your head around something that is brand new to you—or, in the worst-case scenario, the zone of believing, for whatever reason, that you have already done your best. In that unfortunate situation, Zone 3 is the place where you take a couple of good swings with the hammer and then head back into the house to watch television. The point is this: if you are not actively striving to make your way into Zone 1, this zone can become the place where you convince yourself you are not capable of, or interested in, learning more, doing any better, or making any more significant contribution than you already have. So unless you are actually LEARNING THE ROPES, which is what I choose to call this quadrant, you run the risk of making this zone a dead end, the place where you choose not to develop your potential. We all pass through this zone on our journey. We just do not want to stop here.

The lower right-hand corner, Zone 4, is where we see low execution standards, meaning little or no desire to improve and adapt over time, accompanied by lots and lots of effort. This is the person who swings away with the hammer for hours on end but never learns anything from mistakes and failure and never improves. Wherever there is massive action without rising standards, wherever there is passion without a desire to grow and learn and contribute more over time, there is a roadblock. This is the zone of learning nothing and desiring to learn nothing. I call it BEATING YOUR HEAD AGAINST THE WALL. Like Zones 2 and 3, it is no crime to land here…but it is a waste of potential and precious time to choose to stay here.

No matter where you happen to be in the Commitment Matrix at any given moment, you get to choose which direction you want to go.

Whether you move toward Zone 1, the Accountability Zone, by swinging THE HAMMER of Commitment, or you slide toward one of the other zones, is a matter of choice—and a matter of action. This is not a question of fate or luck, of some people getting good breaks and other people getting bad breaks. This is up to you. You can make a conscious decision about the Experience into which you are stepping. You can then make a conscious decision to step into an Accountable Mindset that supports that Experience. You can then move out of your comfort zone by taking *massive action* in support of the Experience you have chosen. In other words, you can stake your claim to a place in the Accountability Zone, and you can spend most of your time there. Or you can stick with what is familiar and drift into one of the other zones. It is entirely up to you.

You do not need to know *how* you are going to reach your ultimate goal when you start swinging the hammer. You just need to make the decision to pick up the hammer and get started.

THE POINT OF EXPONENTIAL RETURNS

When you make the decision to keep on swinging the hammer of Commitment, something remarkable happens. You reach a point where the positive outcomes you deliver start to explode in both number and quality. But there is a catch: you have to swing the hammer long enough and consistently enough to get you past the point where most other people give up.

You keep right on swinging the hammer until you get past the point where other people would have looked at the results and said, "You know what, this isn't happening as fast or as big or as dramatically as I wanted it to. I'm not doing this anymore." Then you hit the Point of Exponential Returns, and your results suddenly go through the roof.

Now, it is easy to talk yourself into putting down the hammer. So the question is, why do some people keep swinging when they are looking at the same mediocre results over the same time period? Because they know their purpose. This means the Experience they choose to step into is clear and compelling, and they are resolute in what they believe—their Mindset.

Most of the time, when you see someone who seems to burst onto the scene in a given area with a sudden outpouring of extraordinary achievement, that person is described as an "overnight success." The graphic I have just shared with you shows you why that is not an accurate label at all. The success did not happen overnight. It had a long history of hammer-swinging behind it. What suddenly became *noticeable,* after a long period of Commitment, was the person's exponential results!

Here is an example of what I mean. When Taylor Swift's self-titled debut album came out in 2008 and went platinum seven times over, her success was so stunning and so unexpected that many people thought of the nineteen-year-old singer-songwriter as an "overnight success." What these people usually overlooked, though, was the fact that Swift and her father (her mentor) had been actively swinging the hammer, pursuing the Experience of a professional career in music for Swift, since 2001—when she was twelve years old! That is when Taylor started playing the guitar, writing songs, and, with her mentor, laying the groundwork for what was to come.

Chapter Twenty-One

Exponential Commitment

"Commitment is an act, not a word."
—Jean-Paul Sartre

WHEN YOU ARE IN ZONE 1, the Accountability Zone™ of the Commitment Matrix, here is what is happening: you are taking intelligent action, you are learning and improving with every action you take, and you are also ramping up and expanding your action plan based on what you just learned. This is true Commitment—what I call Exponential Commitment.

- Exponential Commitment accelerates your progress toward the right Experience—the future you are aiming to create.

- Exponential Commitment accelerates and strengthens the three Accountable Mindsets: Gratitude, Respect, and Abundance.

- Exponential Commitment deepens your relationships with the people you serve.

There is a special power to this kind of Commitment. It carries you along. It takes you where you need to go next. It is like an unseen river that is always moving you forward.

> Exponential Commitment carries you along. It takes you where you need to go next. It is like an unseen river that is always moving you forward.

THE JET STREAM

Jet streams are narrow bands of strong, warm wind that tend to blow from west to east all across the globe. If you are flying an airplane and your route happens to be from west to east, it is a good idea to know where the jet streams are, because once you know, you can use the momentum of the jet stream to your journey's advantage.

You may not always know that it is there, but the jet stream is going to get you to your destination faster than you would get there without it! That is what Exponential Commitment is like: guiding your plane into a jet stream. When you take consistent action that aligns with your purpose, when you learn from every action you take, and when you make a habit of finding ways to expand your action plan, things start to happen. Your competencies move up to a new level. New opportunities become easier to notice. And your results bring you closer and closer to the Experience you are creating for yourself and others.

THE OPPOSITE OF FEAR

Exponential Commitment is the opposite of fear.

Exponential Commitment is the opposite of fear.

Ask yourself: *What would the process of moving away from fear and toward Exponential Commitment look like in action?* Well, if you were John F. Kennedy and you were running for Congress in 1946, petrified of the idea of giving a speech in front of a group, the process might begin with you noticing that there is a problem. Here is how one observer described Kennedy's speaking style at the time:

"[Kennedy's] early speeches…were read from a prepared text with all the insecurity of a novice, in a voice 'tensely high-pitched' and 'with a quality of grave seriousness that masked his discomfiture…. He seemed to be just a trifle embarrassed on stage.'"[5]

Then came a decision—the decision to spend time with a mentor (in this case, the candidate's father)—and create a new possibility, a new Experience, an Experience rooted in the desire to become a great speaker. Kennedy wanted to reach his full potential in that arena, and with his father serving as his mentor, he set about creating the road-map for improvement that would get him to that destination.

Then Kennedy made an effort. He took relentless action.

He took the thing that had frightened him most—speaking before a group—and he built his whole world around it. He was up at six in

---

5. Robert Caro, *The Years of Lyndon Johnson: The Passage of Power* (New York: Vintage, 2012), 41.

the morning talking to voters in all imaginable settings. He delivered speech after speech after speech, taking careful note of all the possible opportunities to improve. He kept this up for weeks and months, delivering speeches before groups that would once have intimidated him but which now became more familiar and less threatening. In addition, he began searching out groups to speak to in what were, back then, untraditional ways:

"Kennedy's regimen quickly became arduous. He woke up around 6:15 in the morning and would be on the streets around 7:00. He often went to the dockyards and factories to shake hands with the workers on their way into work. …Kennedy traveled all over the district meeting voters. Dave Powers (a senior aide) recalled that after shaking thousands of dock workers' hands in the morning, Kennedy would then walk up Bunker Hill Street knocking on every door in that three-decker neighborhood. …Kennedy worked hard and brought his methods to every possible home in the district. He climbed creaking tenement stairs to knock on back doors and sat down in kitchens with voters. …In addition, Kennedy went to the barber shops, the delis, bars, pool halls, and any other place that voters might be. In many instances, Kennedy would simply travel the streets shaking hands and talking to voters. Anywhere that people were gathered for any reason, you'd see Mr. Kennedy."[6]

This was Kennedy swinging away with the hammer, improving his technique with every swing. It worked. He improved dramatically as a speaker, won the primary, won the election, and launched one of the twentieth century's most celebrated public service careers. All because he was willing to take relentless action—and make an effort.

---

6.   Seth M. Ridinger, "John F. Kennedy: Public Perception and Campaign Strategy in 1946," *Historical Journal of Massachusetts* 41, no. 2 (Summer 2013), 118–19.

Chapter Twenty-Two

Put Your Commitment Where Your Mouth Is!

"You are what you do, not what you say you'll do." —Carl Jung

TALK IS CHEAP. Commitment shows up in action, not talk. Accountable leaders never mistake talk for action.

> Accountable leaders never mistake talk for action.

Let me give you a classic example of what cheap talk looks like so you can avoid it—and so you can choose Commitment instead.

Many companies have reached a point where their leadership realizes that they are "supposed to" have a summary of company values that they can share with employees, customers, and the media. So what do the leaders at these companies do? They take a look at some *other* company's list of stated values, or maybe a couple of different companies' values. Then, after spending half an hour or so on the Internet, they cut and paste the values that sound best into their own document, print that document out, and post it in the break room. Basically, they treat the identification of the company values as a public relations exercise and as a means of manipulating the employees into believing that they work in one kind of company, when in fact they do not. Putting values on the wall or on your website does not make them real. Making an effort to identify and act in accordance with your unique values is what makes them real.

One of the items that almost always shows up on a cut-and-pasted list is some variation of the following:

Our people are our most important resource. We are committed to their growth and development.

Are you? What action reflects that commitment? Where is this value consistently showing up? Hint: Putting a piece of paper on a bulletin board does not count.

Let's stop and think for a moment about what being truly committed to a direct report's growth and development looks like. I have done plenty of work with companies that live this value and fulfill this Commitment. Here is *one* example—not the only possible example, but one example—of what that value looks like when people are committed to living it: Leaders meet weekly, for an uninterrupted hour, with each of their direct reports to find out what is going on in their lives. This is not a discussion about the leader's priorities, and it is not a discussion about the to-do list. This is a discussion about what is happening in the direct report's world: the kinds of issues this person is dealing with at home, what they are struggling with on the job, what they are proud of in either or both worlds—everything, in short, that the direct report feels comfortable sharing. They may, of course, discuss obstacles to effectiveness in the workplace that the direct reports see, but whatever they discuss is driven by the direct report, not the leader. The leader is sincerely interested in helping their people grow and be their best in everything that is real in their life. And that means listening. For an hour. Once a week.

When I share this example with some leaders who are just learning about accountability, here is what I hear:

An hour? For each direct report? You've got to be kidding. I don't have time for that.

Here is the point. If you say you value the growth and development of your people, *your action has to back that up.*

> **If you say you value the growth and development of your people, your action has to back that up.**

I have worked with companies that redesigned their entire organizational structure so as to make it possible for people to have no more than five direct reports so that they could all have the time and attention necessary to focus on those direct reports as human beings, learn where they are, learn where they want to go, and help them to get there. Maybe that is not what you want to do at your organization, but if you truly are committed to the development of your team members, it is time to ask a big question: *What **are** you going to do?*

Either back up the talk with action or do not say you are committed to the value! Do not lie to people. If supporting your team members really *is* what you believe in, then make an effort—take relentless action. Show your people exactly how committed you are to stepping it up. Find a way to fulfill that Commitment, take a different set of actions, and you will get a different result.

Too many leaders talk the talk and never back it up with action. That is a recipe for disengagement, cynicism, resentment, and, eventually, dysfunction. Accountable leaders take action on what they say they believe! They know they have not actually taken on the belief *until* they take action!

Is there a cost to backing up your belief with action? The answer is yes. There is a cost. Is there a return? The answer is yes there, too. The greatest cost is typically realized in the short term, and the greatest return or gain is always realized in the long term.

> Is there a cost to backing up your belief with action? The answer is yes. There is a cost. Is there a return? The answer is yes there, too. The greatest cost is typically realized in the short term, and the greatest return or gain is always realized in the long term.

Chapter Twenty-Three

How Big a Life
Do You Want to Lead?

"The ethics of excellence are grounded in action." —Price Pritchett

THE SIZE OF THE LIFE YOU LEAD, the size of the impact you have, the size of the Experience you create, is ultimately a function of the size of your Commitment.

> The size of the life you lead, the size of the impact you have, the size of the Experience you create, is ultimately a function of the size of your Commitment.

Want to lead a bigger life? Start swinging a bigger hammer. Make a bigger Commitment.

Let me give you an illustration of how this might play out. Let's say the Experience you have chosen to step into is called *reaching my optimum physical condition.* The outcome you have created is reaching the best possible physical condition you can. The Mindsets you have consciously chosen to embrace for this Experience are Gratitude and Abundance. What does that look like? Well, the right Mindset might start with acknowledging that you live in a time and place where you have access to the resources you need to work out in a way that energizes you, and with you feeling thankful for that reality. That is Gratitude. And your Mindset might also embrace the recognition that you really do *have* all those resources at your disposal—food, drink, training time, guidance from a mentor, support from family and friends—and the assumption that more resources are coming your way without you even having to think about them. That is Abundance. So now: What do you do? What level of Commitment do you have?

Let's do a close-up on what I would call Level 2 Commitment. We will skip right over Level 1 since that is doing the absolute bare minimum and I know that is not where you want to check in on this, given the fact that you have made it this far in the book. Let me be clear: there is absolutely nothing wrong with Level 2. Here is what it looks like:

Level 2 Commitment: You get up in the morning; you go out and run two or three miles. You do that two or three times a week. You keep that up for a month. At the end of the month, you notice that you have developed a certain level of fitness, stamina, and speed—a level that is noticeably and measurably improved from where you were in all three areas when you started out. You run a local 5K race, and you actually finish. That is a first for you.

LEVEL 2 COMMITMENT IS LIKE A TWO-POUND HAMMER.

You can think of the Level 2 Commitment as being like a two-pound hammer. Swinging it consistently delivers *consistently* more powerful outcomes. Let's say that that two-pound hammer delivers an impact of four pounds per square inch. How many nails do you want to drive? What kind of house do you want to build with that hammer? Remember, Commitment has an exponential impact on your results, because you are taking relentless, consistent action. Even small increases in Commitment can have a major impact on the future you are creating.

As I said, I have no problem at all with Level 2, because it is a good place to be, especially if you started out at Level 0 or Level 1. But here is the question: Is it a good place for you to *stay*? You decide the answer to that question is NO. You want to lead a bigger life than that. So you start asking yourself: *What would happen if I doubled my commitment? Is that even possible?*

Of course it is. Here is what your routine looks like when you swing a bigger hammer and move up to Commitment Level 4:

Level 4 Commitment: You want to get even faster, have even better stamina, and be in even better condition. So you double down. Instead of getting up early to run two or three times a week, you get up early to run five days a week. And you decide it is not enough to run two or three miles; you need to run four to six miles. You keep that up for a month. At the end of the month, you notice that your average pace is improving. You are able to run faster, and you are able to run farther. When you run local 5K races, you are finishing with more people behind you than in front of you. That feels great.

THE LEVEL 4 COMMITMENT IS LIKE A FOUR-POUND HAMMER. IT DWARFS THE LEVEL 2 COMMITMENT.

Notice that the Level 4 hammer is twice as heavy as the Level 2 hammer—however, the impact is *exponentially* more powerful. We can think of this hammer as delivering sixteen pounds of pressure per square inch. I use this example to illustrate the exponential force of expanding your Commitment. The results you generate expand with extraordinary speed!

At this stage, you are beginning to see what is possible—and possibility does not stop at Level 4. You could step this up again. In fact, you could *double* your Commitment again. And that is what you decide to do. You update the Experience you want to step into: now you want to run a marathon, and you are willing to double up your level of Commitment to make that happen.

This is what life looks like for you at Level 8 Commitment:

Level 8 Commitment: You do research. You talk to people who are running marathons. You find out how they got started. You find out what worked for them and what did not. You find one or two key books that are regarded as state of the art when it comes to giving advice on training for and running a marathon. You read those books. You put what you learn into practice. You are now consistently running six days a week. If you are not running on a given day, that means you are working on your race plan. You know you need a detailed plan; you also know that as part of that plan, you need to give your body a day off once in a while—a recovery day. You are purposely resting your body from the workout that you had the day before and preparing for the workout to come. Another part of that plan is that there are some days you run long distances at a slower pace, on city streets, and some days when you run on the track doing quarter-mile repeats or mile repeats. This builds up your stamina for the end of the marathon. Whereas before you were running twenty-five miles a week, now you are running between fifty and seventy miles a week, and you are comparing notes on your performance with your accountability partners. You are helping each other to improve. And you DO improve. Five months in, you achieve a goal you once would have thought impossible: you finish a marathon. And you start wondering: If you doubled your commitment yet again…could you win one?

THE LEVEL 8 COMMITMENT IS LIKE AN EIGHT-POUND HAMMER.

When you hit a nail with an eight-pound hammer, you get a dramatically different outcome than you would if you hit the nail with a four-pound hammer. Your results dramatically expand again! Now it is as though you are delivering sixty-four pounds of force per square inch.

Here is the point. Some pursuits in life call for a Level 2 Commitment. And that is fine. But there are other pursuits we find ourselves dealing with that are more important—and these may require a Level

4 Commitment. We need a bigger hammer in those situations. And every once in a while, we realize that we are looking at a pursuit that demands Level 8 or above from us—which means we need to start swinging a bigger hammer than we have ever swung before.

It is our job to know the difference. We must identify, and fulfill, the right level of Commitment for what is in front of us at any given moment.

The greater the Experience we are stepping into, the more important it is to sustain the right Mindset and the greater the Commitment needed to bring it about.

The greater the Experience we are stepping into, the more important it is to sustain the right Mindset and the greater the Commitment needed to bring it about.

Chapter Twenty-Four

Who Are You, Really?

"Be yourself; everyone else is already taken." —Oscar Wilde

ACCOUNTABLE PEOPLE never tire of asking themselves a tough question: *Who am I, really?*

They know the answer to that question is always going to be rooted, not in what they say about themselves, but in the *Commitments* they take on and the *actions* that they choose to take in support of those Commitments.

Our actions do one of two things: they either demonstrate full Commitment to our chosen purpose in life...or they demonstrate Commitment to something else.

> Our actions do one of two things: they either demonstrate full Commitment to our chosen purpose in life...or they demonstrate Commitment to something else.

Recently, I was talking to one of my clients. I'll call her Ellen. I asked Ellen how she had put into practice some of the principles I had shared with her and what the main difference in her life was now, compared to before she began working with me. Her answer was immediate and impassioned: "Now, I use my mission in all aspects of my life to empower people."

When I asked her to give me an example, she said, "I had a tough conversation the other day with someone I was working with. I was giving him some coaching that I knew would help him to step up his game and make a lasting positive impact, but he wasn't following my lead. So at a certain point, I just looked him straight in the eye and told him, 'Listen, this is my mission: *I inspire greatness in people so that they can leave a legacy they can be proud of.* That's who I am. Now, you can go your own way if you want, and that's okay, but I really do want to work with you, and if that's what you choose, then you need to know that us working together means changing some behaviors. So you have a decision to make.' He thought about what I had said, and he eventually came around. He took on my coaching, and he saw some major positive changes in his life."

That is what Commitment looks like. That is action aligned with purpose. Ellen faced a choice: she could step away and say nothing when she encountered that client's ambivalence about her coaching, or she could take action that aligned with her purpose. She chose to take action. *In the moment she took action in support of her purpose, Ellen was her truest self—the person she was meant to be.*

I tell all my students: "*Who you are is the action you take in support of your purpose.*"

> Who you are is the action you take
> in support of your purpose.

That is a high standard, and it is one I have to remind myself constantly to live up to, but it is reality. When we step away from our purpose, when we fail to take action to support that purpose, we step away from the possibility of living life as the person we are meant to be.

If we say we are committed to inspiring greatness in people but we have no actions we can point to that support that goal, are we really committed? If we say we believe in helping people create a legacy but we are not actually doing anything that makes that happen, is that really what we believe? It is our actions, not our words, that identify what we truly believe, and it is our actions that define us as human beings. If we know what our purpose in life is, then it is our duty to take action in support of that purpose. And if we do not yet know what that purpose is, then it is our duty to find out, so we can identify, and take action to prove, who we really are.

Chapter Twenty-Five

Put What You Have Learned about the "c" in $E=mc^2$ into Practice!

"Just do it." —Nike

NOW THAT YOU HAVE LEARNED about Commitment, you are ready to take the next step. Here are some powerful questions about Commitment for you to consider. The more detailed your answers, the better prepared you will be to put what you know into practice.

- What is the most important Experience you have chosen to step into? (Recall that you selected an Experience in Part Two of this book.) Be specific.

- What will it look, feel, and sound like when this Experience takes place?

- What impact will this Experience have on your life and the lives of others? How does it serve people? Whom does it serve?

- How does this Experience support your purpose?

Before you answer, consider once again these wise words from Jackie Robinson: "A life is not important except in the impact it has on other lives." So: What positive impact does your Experience have on the lives of others?

- What is one Accountable Mindset you have adopted in support of this Experience? Again, be specific. Identify a particular challenge that you face regularly, and then identify what you believe about that challenge.

The answer you come up with should connect to a consciously cultivated Mindset of Abundance, Gratitude, and/or Respect that allows you to live your purpose and the Experience it connects to. Remember: You are either embracing a Toxic Mindset or an Accountable Mindset. There is no in-between.

- What *action* have you taken over the past twenty-four hours that supports your Commitment to the Mindset you identified and the Experience you are creating?

Be just as specific here. The action you identify should be something you can measure. For example, if you are a business leader committed to serving by valuing employees and building a great organization: "I invested two hours of one-on-one time, and as a direct result, I got to know two of my direct reports a lot better yesterday. I now know much more about their values, their goals, and their aspirations, and how those align with the company's values and goals." *If you say that you value people but you are not willing to back those words up with action, you do not value what you say you value.*

- Double-check: Does the action you identified connect to your purpose? How do you know? Remember: *Who you are is the action you take in support of your purpose!*

- Whom, specifically, does your purpose serve?

- How does your action support the purpose of serving them?

- Does the action you identified violate the rights of others? If so, it is NOT aligned with the Mindset of Gratitude and it is NOT Accountable.

- Does the action you identified engage you and inspire you to do more, achieve more, and contribute more?

- What specific action pattern have you undertaken that proves you are *relentless* in sustaining the Mindset and achieving the Experience you have identified?

You will know that your action and your Commitment line up with your purpose when they are *relentless!*

Chapter Twenty-Six

The Values Factor

"Open your arms to change, but don't let go of your values." —The Dalai Lama

WHAT I HAVE SHARED with you in this book, what I am urging you to take on and make part of your life going forward, will feel like a stretch…at first.

The Theory of Accountability is as real as you choose to make it. If you use it, it works. It is no exaggeration to say that this simple formula, $E=mc^2$, can transform your life. It will empower you to *create* the life you want for yourself, your family, and the world around you. All you have to do is use it over and over again as you identify and step into one experience after another. What you will find over time is that the experiences you envision and create will grow in both meaning and impact. What seemed impossible just a short time ago will soon become second nature for you. You can become an Accountability Master using this formula to create radical changes not only in what you see as possible, but in what *does* become possible for you.

But this means moving into the Accountability Zone™. It means leaving behind what is comfortable and familiar to you right now. It means making an effort…and taking the time to figure out whether what you are doing can be improved.

Getting clarity on the purpose that defines who you are truly meant to be, the mission that motivates you and attracts others, and the Experience that creates the future you want to live will take some effort in the beginning. It will feel like a bit of a stretch…at first.

Noticing when you are in a Toxic Mindset and making the conscious decision to flip that around to an Accountable Mindset will also take some practice. It will not feel natural to you at the outset, because you may have spent a good portion of your life thus far not noticing your Mindset or its impact on your relationships with others. Assuming control of this part of your life will feel like a bit of a stretch…at first.

And upping your level of Commitment so that you are truly relentless in executing your game plan may not feel easy the first few times you try to move beyond your comfort zone. This, too, will feel like a bit of a stretch…at first.

All three parts of the equation that make up the Theory of Accountability come with a learning curve.

Here is my best advice for condensing that learning curve: *figure out what your values are.*

Our character is either one created by design, where we have taken the time to think about what we believe and value, what those values mean to us, why they are worth protecting, and how our values show up in our daily life…or we have a character by default, and we do none of that. In the latter case, we follow the path of least resistance. Avoid that path. Identify what matters most to you in life. Is it service? Contribution? Integrity? (If you would like some assistance, download my free Values Worksheet at www.samsilverstein.com/valuesworksheet.) Then, when you discover your values, keep an eye out for mentors and accountability partners whose values you are absolutely certain align with yours, connect with them, and share with them the Experience you are working to create.

> Identify what matters most to you in life. Is it service? Contribution? Integrity? Once you discover your values, keep an eye out for mentors and accountability partners whose values you are absolutely certain align with yours.

By doing this, you will leverage what I call the Values Factor. If you keep aligning what you are doing with the values that are most important to you and you receive continued support from people who share your values, you will find that the learning curve compresses, the journey toward mastery becomes easier, and the results you achieve become exponentially greater. When you live your values with every action and every decision consistently over time, you will see that the results you create for yourself and others are enormous.

I will close this book with three big ideas for you to consider as you move forward:

Who you are is the action you take in support of your purpose. At any given moment, you are either choosing to live that purpose or choosing to step away from it. Choose the former.

Create an Experience that will outlive you. The bigger and more long-lasting the positive impact your Experience has on the larger world, the more fulfilled you will be.

Pass it on. In these pages I have emphasized, over and over again, how important it is to have a mentor. My final challenge to you is to *be* a mentor to someone else. Help someone to see and create an

Experience they think they are incapable of creating…and then help them to make that a reality. Put a stake in the ground. To be our very best self, we have to allow others into our life as mentors, because they see things about our own potential that we may not. We will never be our best self unless we are serving others. The act of serving others, in and of itself, elevates us, and one of the best ways to serve is to be a mentor for someone who can benefit from that. There is always someone a mile ahead of us; there is always someone a mile behind us. Do not forget to help others tap into what they are capable of. Be an advocate for them becoming all that they can be. Then challenge them to do the same for someone who is a mile behind *them*. Leave a legacy of accountability. That is the best legacy there is.

> **Pass it on. Leave a legacy of accountability. That is the best legacy there is.**

Appendix

Summary of Accountability Points from This Book

POST ONE OR MORE OF THESE Accountability Points where you can see them each and every day!

If we want to make accountability a daily reality in our life, in our team, and in our organization, we must change the way we think.

Tactical commitments are not enough. If there is no relational commitment anywhere, then there is no accountability.

The Experience we create is the result of the Mindset we embrace and the exponential impact of our Commitment.
Or: $E = mc^2$

Creating the Experience is the foundation of accountability, and it takes practice. For most of us, it also takes outside help.

All too often, we create a limited Experience for ourselves and those in our circle.

Mentors know when to push you beyond your comfort zone.

Create a future that benefits others, not just yourself.

Where there is a strong organizational culture of mentorship, there is a strong culture of accountability.

Your future is emerging at this instant.

It will likely take time and practice to learn to set your own course, to learn to take personal control of your future.

The steeper the hill you are heading down, the more you lean into it. While that may seem counterintuitive, that's the only way to survive a steep incline—by leaning into it and making sure you stay in control.

We each have a choice about the kind of future we want to create for ourselves and the larger world.

We will never reach our full potential by following the path of least resistance.

The Moment of Truth is the moment you choose to move beyond what is comfortable to create a whole different reality, a whole different future.

Creating the Experience requires a conversation with someone else. If you have not talked about the future you are creating with another human being, you are not creating the Experience.

The Moment of Truth is a powerful moment. It always propels us forward, toward a decision that creates a newer and fuller expression of the person we are meant to be.

The future you choose to create has to be connected to your very best self. We become our best selves only when we allow someone to help us—and when we are helping someone else to become their best self.

What we allow in our space, we condone.

An excuse is a story you tell yourself to sell yourself and try to sell to others.

Each of us faces Moments of Truth that are unique to us.

Making a purposeful decision is how we create the future.

Creating the Experience means embracing our purpose and then stepping into the future that matches up with that purpose...even when that purpose points us toward a future we do not yet believe we are capable of creating.

Our purpose speaks to us and becomes more obvious in Moments of Truth.

Create an Experience that will outlive you!

Your mission is your purpose in action.

Our unique purpose is the service at the heart of our life that inspires us, fulfills us, and clarifies who we are meant to be.

Purpose and mission are the tools we use to create our Experience, the future we choose to step into.

Invest the time necessary to get a clear sense of your purpose in life.

Every decision you make—every single one—interacts with your purpose. It either supports that purpose or it does not.

If you believe you have found your purpose, but your purpose does not connect in any way to serving another person, keep looking!

Happiness is a construct, one that, for the most part, is created by other people.

Happiness is fleeting; fulfillment endures.

Sooner or later we figure out that only one thing actually leaves us feeling fulfilled—pursuing our purpose.

We all have the power to use our decisions to create a future that we believe is worth living.

At any given moment, we are each creating the future that we are about to experience.

The only antidote to excuses is to refocus, with intensity, on those things you can control in your life that connect to your purpose.

Your Mindset is what you believe at any given moment.

What you believe about your world drives the action you take to create that world.

If our actions do not support a stated belief, we do not hold that belief. And we need to notice that.

People who live in the Gratitude Mindset know that everyone and everything is connected.

There is something special that happens when you give, and give freely.

People who live in an Abundance Mindset make a point of sharing freely of their time, their talents, and their treasures—meaning all their available resources.

When we consider another human being solely as a means to an end—our end—and we treat them accordingly, we are locked into the Toxic Mindset of Contempt.

As soon as we pass judgment on another person, our respect for that person vanishes and contempt takes over.

People who live in a Respect Mindset accept that every viewpoint matters, even if it is not one they happen to share.

If we choose to step into a Respect Mindset, we will not have a Contempt Mindset. If we choose to step into an Abundance Mindset, we will not have a Scarcity Mindset. If we choose to step into a Gratitude Mindset, we will not have an Entitlement Mindset.

Making toxicity our default setting is all too easy, especially if the people around us are making a habit of using one or more of the three Toxic Mindsets. Choose to surround yourself with people who embrace the Accountable Mindsets.

Toxic Mindsets are not healthy, no matter how easy it may be for us to slip into using them. Accountable Mindsets always lead us in the right direction.

Toxic Mindsets are easy—and destructive. Accountable Mindsets take practice—and they strengthen relationships.

It is always up to us to notice whether the Mindset we have chosen to step into is Accountable or Toxic, just like it is always up to us which direction a car is headed when we are driving it.

The trick is not simply to "think positively" but to be aware of what we are thinking.

There are three, and only three, Accountable Mindsets. The flip side of each Accountable Mindset is a Toxic Mindset. This means there are three Mindset Transitions that accountable people learn to make:

TOXIC	→	ACCOUNTABLE
SCARCITY	→	ABUNDANCE
ENTITLEMENT	→	GRATITUDE
CONTEMPT	→	RESPECT

We are responsible for every single outcome in our lives—no exceptions. If we want different outcomes, we have to change what we BELIEVE about a given person, a given situation, or a given opportunity from Toxic to Accountable. That means changing our Mindset and thereby changing our actions.

To adopt an Accountable Mindset, we need to make the transition from self to service.

Commitment is taking action in a purposeful way, repeatedly and relentlessly.

Commitment is the hammer. Keep the hammer swinging!

Exponential Commitment carries you along. It takes you where you need to go next. It is like an unseen river that is always moving you forward.

Exponential Commitment is the opposite of fear.

Accountable leaders never mistake talk for action.

If you say you value the growth and development of your people, your action has to back that up.

Is there a cost to backing up your belief with action? The answer is yes. There is a cost. Is there a return? The answer is yes there, too. The greatest cost is typically realized in the short term, and the greatest return or gain is always realized in the long term.

The size of the life you lead, the size of the impact you have, the size of the Experience you create, is ultimately a function of the size of your Commitment.

The greater the Experience we are stepping into, the more important it is to sustain the right Mindset and the greater the Commitment needed to bring it about.

Our actions do one of two things: they either demonstrate full Commitment to our chosen purpose in life...or they demonstrate Commitment to something else.

Who you are is the action you take in support of your purpose.

Identify what matters most to you in life. Is it service? Contribution? Integrity? Once you discover your values, keep an eye out for mentors and accountability partners whose values you are absolutely certain align with yours.

Pass it on. Leave a legacy of accountability. That is the best legacy there is.

ABOUT THE AUTHOR

SAM SILVERSTEIN is founder and CEO of Sam Silverstein, Incorporated, an accountability think tank dedicated to helping companies create an organizational culture that prioritizes and inspires accountable leaders. By helping organizations develop what they believe in, clarify their mission, and understand what is in their control, Sam works to make this a more accountable world. He is the author of several books, including *No More Excuses, Non-Negotiable, No Matter What, The Success Model, Making Accountable Decisions, The Lost Commandments,* and *I Am Accountable.* He speaks internationally, having worked with teams of companies, government agencies, communities, and organizations both big and small, including Kraft Foods, Pfizer, the United States Air Force, and United Way. Sam is the past president of the National Speakers Association.

Book Sam Silverstein
To Speak At Your Next Event

Contact Us

Sam Silverstein, Incorporated
121 Bellington Lane
St. Louis, Missouri 63141
info@SamSilverstein.com
(314) 878-9252

To Order More Copies of
The Theory of Accountability

www.samsilverstein.com

Follow Sam

www.twitter.com/samsilverstein

www.youtube.com/samsilverstein

www.linkedin.com/in/samsilverstein

www.instagram.com/samsilverstein

www.facebook.com/silversteinsam

No More Excuses | Making Accountable Decisions | The Success Model | I Am Accountable

OTHER BOOKS BY
SAM SILVERSTEIN
AVAILABLE EVERYWHERE
BOOKS ARE SOLD or
www.SamSilverstein.com

The Accountability Circle

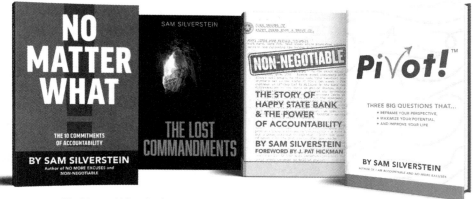

No Matter What | The Lost Commandments | Non Negotiable | Pivot!